A Collection of Restaurant Recipes
from the Queen City of the Ozarks

This fundraiser cookbook features over 200 delicious recipes
that were donated by some of the best independent and locally owned
restaurants in Springfield, Missouri.

Some of Springfield's elite businesses helped to sponsor the publishing
and promotion of this wonderful cookbook.

Proceeds from the sale of these cookbooks will go to benefit
Springfield's Urban Districts Alliance.

Enjoy!

Special Thanks from the Editor:
This cookbook would not have been possible without the support from all the restaurant owners, chefs and sponsors who appear in this book.

Library of Congress Control Number: 2008933519

ISBN: 978-0-9816282-2-6

Published by:
JEC Publishing Company
2049 East Cherry Street, Suite 100
Springfield, Missouri 65802
(800) 313-5121

Editor: JE Cornwell
Editorial Coordinator: Pam Eddings
Graphics Layout: Tom Dease
Graphics Contribution: Liz Russell
Cover Design: Andy Cobb

Printed in China

Publication name; *Taste of Springfield Cookbook -A Collection of Restaurant Recipes from the Queen City of the Ozarks*, is the property of Recipe Publishers.

Foreword

On behalf of the Urban Districts Alliance, welcome to the second annual Taste of Springfield! This event far exceeded our expectations last year with 5,000 people in attendance. This inaugural Taste of Springfield cookbook builds on that success and celebrates the lively culinary arts in Center City with recipes from skilled professionals as well as downtown devotees.

You may ask, as many do, what is UDA? It is a non-profit community development corporation providing leadership, programs, and services to preserve and strengthen the economic vitality of Center City and each of its distinctive historic business districts. Eleven years ago, I was honored to be asked to participate in the formation of this vital organization, which has brought energy, commitment and strength to the revitalization of our Center City, working through its three commercial districts -- Downtown, Historic Walnut Street, and Commercial Street.

The idea for UDA came from a desire for an organization to unite the three districts under one board and staff for maximum efficiency and impact. The Board of Directors was and still is composed of major stake-holders in the revitalization effort. (Go to www.itsalldowntown.com/UDA for additional information on the UDA).

Collaboration is the name of the game in Center City and UDA has many partnerships and relationships for the Taste of Springfield, including -- Banta Foods, St. John's Foundation, Hoover Music Company, the Downtown Community Improvement District, Downtown Springfield Association, the Ozarks Regional YMCA, and dozens of volunteers.

Serving as the "keeper of the flame" -- the vision of a revitalized urban core brought about by organizations and individuals united in that mission -- is another way to describe UDA. As you sample some of Springfield's best dining, music, art, and shopping, we welcome you to join UDA and all its partners in that exciting journey!

Jan Horton

Center City Organizations

Urban Districts Alliance (UDA)

Formed in 1997 as a recommendation by Vision 20/20, serves as an umbrella organization to coordinate and consolidate all Center City organizations into one cooperative effort. The board is composed of representatives from each of the districts and organizations Downtown Springfield Association, Springfield Finance and Development Corporation, Springfield Regional Arts Council, Historic Walnut Street Association, Commercial Club, plus the Springfield Area Chamber of Commerce, City of Springfield, Springfield City Council, Greene County, City Utilities, Drury University, Ozarks Technical Community College, Missouri State University, along with representation from developers and other interested parties. Contact Rusty Worley, UDA Executive Director (417-831-6200 or rusty@itsalldowntown.com), for additional information.

Community Improvement District (CID)

"Creating a cleaner, safer, and more vibrant downtown."

The CID was established in 1999 by property owners within a specific geographic boundary (Elm Street on the south, Main Avenue on the west, Water Street on the north, and Kimbrough on the east) to provide supplemental services for maintenance, parking enforcement and image enhancement. Examples of these services include:

- Daily cleaning of sidewalks and public parking lots.
- Power washing sidewalks.
- Administering the Parking Ambassador staff and public parking program.
- Installing of District banners.
- Coordinating a FREE Wi-Fi pilot project with the City, Greene County and City Utilities.
- Managing the itsalldowntown.com website.
- Encouraging community and retail events to bring new patrons to the District.

CID is currently funded by property assessments and voluntary contributions. A new revenue source – a quarter cent sales tax was voted on and on February 27th the registered voters who live in the CID district approved a quarter-cents sales tax initiative. The sales tax is scheduled to begin on July 1, 2007 and will be collected by merchants, restaurants, and other businesses currently charging sales tax in the CID district.

The CID was extended another ten years in the fall of 2006. The District contracts the Urban Districts Alliance to provide day-to-day management for its programs.

Please contact Barb Baker, CID Manager, at 417-831-6200 or barb@itsalldowntown.com for additional information.

Downtown Springfield Association (DSA)

"Serving the heart of the city by improving and promoting the diverse historic, cultural, social and economic environment of downtown Springfield." Formed in 1965, DSA is a volunteer-driven membership-based organization funded by member participation and events. Its mission includes business development and projects to draw new customers and business prospects to downtown. The DSA also works with other downtown organizations in a collaborative effort to support and promote business downtown. Major DSA programs include downtown capital and infrastructure improvement prioritization and implementation, networking socials, and major retail events such as Sidewalk sales, holiday open houses and the Downtown Discount Card program. If you are interested in joining the DSA as a Visionary Member ($500 yearly), a Civic Member ($150 yearly) or as on individual at the Advocate level ($50) please contact Kathryn at kathryn@itsalldowntown.com or call 417.831.6200 for additional information.

continued on next page

Commercial Street

Among the hip lofts and ornate brick-work facades of buildings built in the late 1800s lies a tight-knit community interested in returning their historic district to its full glory.

Volunteer-driven and membership-based, the Commercial Club is a non-profit organization that focuses its attention on Center City's northern neighborhood through planning and sponsorship of special events, a farmer's market and supporting the beautification of district landmarks, like the Jefferson Avenue Footbridge.

Commercial Club is also responsible for facilitating the design and implementation of street scape improvements in the Commercial Street historic district.

The district is known for its eclectic retail mix and is listed on the National Register of Historic Places. The district is located between Lyon and Washington Streets.

Visible in everything they do, Commercial Club's purpose is simply to promote the historic aspects of their district, promote business, and facilitate cooperation between their business district and the surrounding neighborhoods.

The club sponsors events for the cosmopolitan in all of us, like the annual Loft Walk, the C-Street Jam Music Festival, and varied smaller events like our Silent Film Summer Series set to live ragtime music and held in the courtyard of historic Fire Station #2.

Visit the street in April through October and you'll find the C-Street Market, a quaint Farmer's Market offering produce, breads, flowers, arts and crafts. Visit http://thecommercialstreetmarket.com/ for vendor listings, links and market schedules.

Or, just come to do a little shopping in our growing selection of shops and businesses.

Commercial Club general membership meetings are held the first Tuesday of every month at 6:00 p.m. on the second floor of our Commercial Club building, 299 E. Commercial Street.

Come. "Rediscover the Treasure of Springfield.

Historic Walnut Street Association

Historic Walnut Street charms visitors with stately manors and fabled gingerbread landmarks that anchor the residential east end and transition to the boutique shops and lodging, offices, restaurants, and apartments toward the west end of the historic district.

Walnut Street serves as the backdrop for two annual festivals--Artsfest and Cider Days. Artsfest centers on artistic creations for public purchase while Cider Days focuses on the arts as well as regional crafts.

From the 1880s to today, Historic Walnut Street is a wonderful place to live, work and play.

The Historic Walnut Street Association (HWSA) represents the property owners, residents and businesses on Historic Walnut Street from Kimbrough Street on the west, to National Avenue on the East, in the heart of old downtown Springfield.

Jordan Valley Marketing Council

This ad-hoc coalition of organizations and entities with an interest in activity in the Jordan Valley Park area focuses on coordination of events and marketing efforts in the area encompassing the Exposition Center and Hammons Field west to downtown. Major programs include Festival of Lights and Concerts in the Park. For more information visit our www.springfieldmo.gov/jvp.

Table of Contents

Contributors

1955 MAPLE CAFE
5 SPICE CHINA GRILL
AN ARTS PATRONAGE INITIATIVE
ANDY'S FROZEN CUSTARD
ANTON'S COFFEE SHOP
ARGENTINA STEAKHOUSE
AVANZARE ITALIAN DINING
BAMBU VIETNAMESE CUISINE
BANTA FOODS
BETH'S BAKE SHOPPE & TEA ROOM
BIG MOMMA'S COFFEE & ESPRESSO BAR
BIG WHISKEYS
BIJAN'S SEA & GRILL
BRUNOS RESTAURANT
CASSILS COFFEE CAFE
CLARY'S RESTAURNAT
COOKS KETTLE RESTAURANT
COUNTRY DELI CAKES-CATERING
COXHEALTH
DRURY UNIVERSITY
EASY'S CAJUN RESTAURANT
EBBETS FIELD RESTAURANT & BAR
ERNIE BIGGS
FEDORAS SOCIAL HOUSE
FIRE & ICE RESTAURANT & BAR
FIRST FRIDAY ART WALK
FIRST NATIONAL BANK
GALLERY BISTRO
GALLOWAY STATION BAR & GRILL
GARY FENTON, CPA
GEM OF INDIA RESTAURANT & BAR
GLOBAL FAYRE
HARRY COOPER SUPPLY CO
HARTER HOUSE
HAWTHORN GALLERIES
HEMINGWAY'S BLUE WATER CAFÈ
HICKOK'S STEAKHOUSE & BREWERY
HONEY HEAVEN
J. BUCKS RESTAURANT
JULIE'S CHEWIES GOURMET COOKIES

JUST GO TO THE PARTY!
KOLR-10 TV STATION
MAMA JEAN'S NATURAL MARKET
MARIA'S MEXICAN RESTAURANT
METRO BUILDERS SUPPLY
METROPOLITAN GRILL
MICHELLE CANTRELL & ASSOC
MILLE'S CAFÈ & BAR
MUDHOUSE
MUTUAL OF OMAHA
NONNA'S ITALIAN AMERICAN CAFÉ
OASIS HOTEL & CONVENTION CNT
OCEAN ZEN
PAPPY'S PLACE
PARLOR 88
PASTICHE DECOR & DESIGN
PATTON ALLEY PUB
PEABODY'S
PLANET SMOOTHIE
PRICE CUTTER
RECIPE PUBLISHERS
RENDEZVOUS COFFEE LOUNGE
RIAD GREEK CUISINE
RICE EQUIPMENT SERVICE
RODIZIO BRAZILIAN GRILL
SPRINGFIELD BREWREY
SPRINGFIELD CARDINALS
SPRINGFIELD NEWS-LEADER
ST. MICHAEL'S
THE COFFEE ETHIC
THE GROTTO
THE HOME BREWERY
TONIC ULTRALOUNGE
TOWER CLUB RESTAURANT
TROLLEY'S BAR & GRILL
TROLLEY'S LEVEL 2
TUSCAN GRILL
URBAN DISTRICTS ALLIANCE
VENICE AT THE SEVILLE
WAVES OF GRAIN

Beverages

Avanzare Italian Dining

1908 S. Glenstone
Springfield, MO 65804
417-567-3463

www.avanzareitaliandining.com

Exceptional Northern Italian cuisine is the center piece of Avanzare. As you dine with us, you'll find world class chef Tony Garcia prepares each dish with only the finest freshly sourced ingredients, including fresh made bread and desserts. A little bit of Italy sits quietly "On the Plaza at Glenstone and Sunshine." Surrounding ourselves with only the best ensures your dining experience at Avanzare is what you anticipate and deserve!

Italian Margarita

1 oz. amaretto
1/2 oz. tequila
Ice cubes

1/2 oz. Cointreau
2 oz. fresh squeezed lime juice

Shake the ingredients with ice and serve 'up' or on the rocks in a salt-rimmed glass. Garnish with a lime wedge.

Italian Coffee

1 c. hot black coffee

2 oz. amaretto

Mix. Top with whipped cream.

Italian Delight

1 oz. amaretto
1-1/2 oz. cream or half & half

1/2 oz. orange Juice

Fill shaker with ice. Add ingredients and shake. Strain into chilled glass. Garnish with cherry.

Submitted by: Wade Sumter, General Manager

Cassils Cafes Inc.

2925 W. Republic Rd.
Springfield, MO 65807
417-851-1104

2601 N. Cresthaven
Springfield, MO 65803
417-866-2221

www.cassils.com

Cassils is your neighborhood gathering place. Whether it's stopping by on the way to work for a latte and fresh cinnamon roll, taking a client to lunch, studying for finals on your laptop, having dinner with your family, or enjoying live entertainment with your friends, Cassils is your place. At Cassils, we started by bringing to Springfield some of the best coffees the world has to offer, roasted and blended by some of the best roasters in the country. We added to that our award-winning menu of unique, casual appetizers, entrees, baked goodies, and desserts. We serve it all up in a comfortable, friendly atmosphere you're going to love.

The World's Best Mocha

2 shots espresso
8 oz. milk

1 oz. chocolate syrup

Start by pulling two shots of espresso into a 16 ounce mug into which you have placed 1 ounce of chocolate syrup. Since the taste of your mocha will depend largely on the quality of your ingredients, we recommend you use a premium espresso (for example those available at Cassils™) and a premium chocolate (we use Ghirardelli). Pour cold milk into a chilled steaming pitcher and carefully steam the milk to a uniform, velvety texture. Immediately pour the steamed milk into the chocolate-espresso mixture. Top with whipped cream, if you like.

Italian Creamosa

1-1/4 oz. flavored syrup
2 oz. half & half

8 oz. soda water
Ice

Fill a 16 ounce glass about 2/3 full of ice cubes. Drizzle the syrup flavors of your choice over the ice. Some favorites are vanilla, strawberry-banana, and raspberry. We recommend you use high quality syrup. The flavor will be more intense without diluting the drink. Add the soda water to within about 1/2 inch of the top of the glass. Pour in the half & half, stir, and enjoy. Humming "O sole mio" while making this drink is entirely optional.

Submitted by: Kevin Cassil, Country-boy, Scientist, and Restaurant Owner

The Coffee Ethic

124 Park Central Square
Springfield, Mo 65806
417-866-6645

www.thecoffeeethic.com

Owners Jim Hamilton and Tom Billionis share the same passion, ideas and believe in an alternative way of doing business. The Coffee Ethic, a for-profit for-good enterprise, based on our belief that business solutions can be used for personal, communal and social transformation. The Coffee Ethic coffee bar is on the square in downtown Springfield, MO. The focus is on single-origin coffee and espresso-based drinks and an offering of locally baked, fresh pastries. The Coffee Ethic sells premium products and fosters community and personal connections by providing a "Third Place". A place where people can go, aside from work and home, that is safe, rich, colorful, and stimulating. The name comes from the Greek "Ethikos", literally translated into modern English as "theory of living". Their theory of living and business is found in the mission statement: Center on the Cup, Value the People, Care for the Earth.

Japanese Iced Coffee

At The Coffee Ethic we are always looking for methods to capture the essence of the coffee(s) and provide the most flavorful experience possible for our customers. One of the non-traditional ways people enjoy coffee these days is over ice. This is a simple way to prepare and enjoy iced coffee at home anytime. This brew method captures all the flavor nuances of a quality coffee that a normal hot brew process would, but it yields a cold, refreshing beverage you will be eager to drink and proud to serve. It's also a favorite of our staff of Baristas.

-Start with a 64 oz. pitcher & fill 3/4-full with large ice cubes.

-Measure and grind 4.25 oz. (adjust to taste) of your favorite coffee. We suggest an East African or Central American coffee with fruity or citrus notes.

-Put the grinds in a brew basket (from your home brewer), using a normal paper filter, on top of the pitcher so it will brew directly on the ice. (Note: a Melitta "pour-over" brewer may be used as well)

-Slowly pour 32 ounces of water (or until total volume in pitcher reaches 64 ounces) at a temperature of around 200 ° (just off the boil) over the grounds.

-As it brews, the ice will melt and immediately cool the coffee while creating the proper brew strength. This will capture the aroma and sweetness of the coffee.

-When the brew process is complete the ice should be mostly melted. It is ready for immediate enjoyment or may be stored in the refrigerator. It will keep its flavor for several days.

-Serve the coffee over additional ice. The Japanese also serve it with simple syrup and chilled heavy cream.

Submitted by: Jim Hamilton, Co-owner

Easy's Cajun Restaurant & Bar

1710 S Glenstone Ave
Springfield, MO 65804
417-881-3939

www.easysrestaurant.com

Easy's
CAJUN RESTAURANT & BAR

If you could turn the colorful trademarks of Mardi Gras into an edible dish, then you might find yourself at Easy's Cajun Restaurant & Bar with its soothing colors, relaxing tables and creative menu items. This family-owned and operated eatery serves each freshly prepared meal with lots of passion. Nothing but the finest ingredients go into the Southern recipes, and although they may be Asian, their hearty comfort food is very much known to be as good or better than some of the restaurants down South. With plenty of entrees and original fusion items, each dish is served hot and fresh with a side of soul.

Sexybacktini

Feature in 417 Magazine 2007 SUMMER GUIDE as a must do!

2 oz. Stoli
1 oz. Hypnotiq
4 oz. Red Bull

1 oz. X-Rated
1 oz. Blue Cuaracao

First put Stoli, X-Rated, and Red Bull in a shaker and shake for 15 seconds. Then pour Hypnotiq and Blue Cuaracao off the side of martini glass so it will float to bottom. Take slice of lemon and squeeze juice; take peel and rub on rim. Use the peel as a twist and drop into martini. The martini should look like a rainbow with a raspberry rim. Garnish with berry rim and cherry on rim.

Submitted by: Kevin Kwok, Executive Chef & Owner

In Loving Memory of Eddie Kwok (Executive Chef) who passed away on November 1, 2007

Fire & Ice Restaurant and Bar

At Oasis Hotel and Convention Center
2546 N. Glenstone
Springfield, MO 65803
417-522-7711

www.oasisfireandice.com

The Oasis Hotel proudly presents Fire & Ice Restaurant & Bar, where an exquisite atmosphere and culinary creativity welcome hotel guests and the general public. Fire & Ice features Springfield's only curved counter-top ice bar, and offers seating that extends to the indoor pool and its surrounding fountains and plant life, as well as seasonal seating around the hotel's outdoor pool. The open-plan kitchen allows patrons to watch a show of flames behind the ice bar performed by Executive Chef Wing Yee Leong and his team as they prepare the evening's entrees. Dinner fare at Fire & Ice includes seafood delights, steak specialties, and a variety of beef, shrimp, and chicken dishes showcasing Chef Wing's mastery of the wok.

Liquid Oasis

3/4 oz. Malibu coconut rum
Orange juice
Rose's grenadine

3/4 oz. Dekuyper Peachtree schnapps
Pineapple juice

Fill hurricane glass with ice and add rum and schnapps. Then fill glass with equal parts orange juice and pineapple juice. Top off the drink with a splash of grenadine to add color. Garnish drink with a slice of pineapple and a cherry.

Chico's Mai Tai

1/2 oz. simple syrup
1 oz. Bacardi Superior light rum
1/4 oz. Myers dark rum
Pineapple juice

1/2 oz. Rose's grenadine
1/4 oz. Bacardi Gold rum
Orange juice

In hurricane glass add simple syrup and grenadine; then add ice. Add light rum. Fill glass with equal parts orange juice and pineapple juice. Float the gold rum and dark rum on top.
Garnish the drink with an orange slice and a cherry.

Submitted by: Wing Yee Leong, Executive Chef

First Friday Art Walk

411 N. Sherman Parkway
Springfield, Missouri 65802
417-849-8255

www.ffaw.org

First Friday Art Walk, held 6-10 p.m. the first Friday of each month, is a free walking tour of downtown Springfield's 20-plus art galleries. The event features works by local, regional and national artists, as well as live demonstrations and performances, all in support of First Friday Art Walk's nonprofit mission of promoting fine art and economic vitality in the Downtown Arts District. For more information, give us a call or visit our website.

Pomegranate Martini

1-1/2 c. 100% Pomegranate juice
1 c. ice
Lime, thin slices

3 oz. Absolut vodka (or favorite citrus flavored vodka)
Splash of tonic

Shake juice, vodka, ice and tonic. Strain into chilled martini glasses. Put thin slice of lime in glasses to garnish. Serves 2.

Black-Eyed Susan

This is a really great recipe from my friends at Pimlico race track.
It is served as the official drink of the Preakness Stakes horse race in Baltimore, MD.

1-1/4 c. vodka
1-1/4 c. light rum
3/4 c. triple sec
4 c. pineapple juice

4 c. orange juice
Ice ring
1 Tbsp. fresh lime juice

Chill all ingredients. Just before serving, combine in a punch bowl. Un-mold ice ring and float in bowl. Serve in tall glasses with cherry, orange slice, and pineapple cube garnish. Makes 10 large servings.

Submitted by: Susan Sommer-Luarca Fine Art Gallery & Frame Shoppe

Gallery Bistro

221 E Walnut St
Springfield, MO 65806
417-866-0555

www.gallerybistrodowntown.com

Gallery Bistro

Gallery Bistro is located on Historic Walnut Street in Downtown Springfield; just two doors down from the Landers Theatre and next to the Vandivort Theatre. Our contemporary cuisine is an eclectic mix of Asian, French, English, Spanish and Down-home. Friendly, attentive and knowledgeable service is our trademark. Combined with our extensive wine collection and massive martini repertoire, our patrons are ensured of a fabulous dining experience. Gallery Bistro is the place to go for dinner or light fare before the show, or after the curtain falls. Late night cocktails and an appetizer - or our famous mushroom sage soup - are favorites of Springfield theater-goers.

Mojito Nuevo

For 10 drinks:

1/2 bottle white rum
1/2 c. club soda or sprite
2 large fresh limes, juiced

2 c. simple syrup
2 large sprigs fresh mint

Crush mint sprig in the bottom of a large pitcher. Add the rum, lime juice and simple syrup and stir well. When ready to serve, add ice and club soda (or sprite) and stir. Garnish the bottom of each iced glass with a small mint sprig and pour Mojito on top. Serve.

Simple syrup for 10 Mojitos:

3/4 c. sugar

2-1/4 c. water

Add the sugar to the water and bring to a boil. Reduce heat and simmer sugar water for three minutes. Remove from heat and allow to cool.

Submitted by: Peter Tinson, Owner & Executive Chef

Global Fayre

324 S Campbell
Springfield, MO 65806
417- 873-9792

www.globalfayre.com

Buying Fair Trade has always been important to us. After our youngest daughter was born, we wanted to find something that we could do together, something that we believed in and that would benefit the wider, global community. We also shared a love of artisan products from Asia, Africa and South America, and so it was a natural choice for us to launch Global Fayre, with the mission of bringing Fair Trade products to southwest Missouri.

Iced Coffee

Each iced coffee method recommended below is suited for light and dark roasts and will bring out the attributes in each coffee.

French Press Method: Use a coarse grind for your coffee. Boil water and set aside for 2 minutes to achieve the proper brew temperature (195-205° F.). Infuse ground coffee with hot water and wait for the coffee to steep for 4-5 minutes.
Brew Time: After the 4-5 minute steep, transfer brewed coffee to a glass or ceramic decanter and leave the brew at room temperature for 6 hours. Then add ice and serve or refrigerate the decanter.
Tasting Notes: The weight and texture of this method is unsurpassed and provides an almost espresso-like consistency. The temperature of the hot water used to brew the coffee is crucial to making a great French press for this iced coffee method. In addition, we found that delaying the transfer of the brewed coffee into another vessel produced a much more bitter cup.

Automatic Home Brewer Method: Use 1 unbleached paper filter, 1 well rounded tablespoon of ground coffee per cup of water and begin brewing.
Brew Time: Brew and leave coffee at room temperature, off the warming plate for 6 hours. Add ice and serve or refrigerate.
Tasting Notes: We found that the flavor produced from a home brewer with a paper filter was superior to that of a gold metal filter. The paper filter produced crisp and bright attributes, while the metal filter muted these same flavors and created an almost stale effect on the coffee. In addition, we strongly recommend using a home brewer with at least 850 watts of power to achieve the proper water temperature for brewing which heavily impacts the way the coffee tastes.

Americano Method: Pour a 1 ounce properly prepared shot of espresso into 3 ounces of cool water and then add ice. Be sure to add the ice last to reduce the temperature shock for the espresso.
Brew Time: 30 seconds
Tasting Notes: This method requires a professional grade espresso machine, but the flavor of the espresso is well preserved and the crema is still intact.

Toddy Method: Using a Toddy brewer, combine 1 pound of ground coffee with 72 ounces of cold water. Let the coffee and water combination stay at room temperature for 24 hours and filter the grounds when the brew cycle is complete.
Brew Time: 12 hours
Tasting Notes: The Toddy method produces a very mellow cup of iced coffee that can be stored as a concentrate for up to two weeks in the refrigerator.

Submitted by: Cheri and David Crump, Owners

The Home Brewery

205 W Bain St
Ozark, MO 65721
417-581-0963

www.homebrewery.com

Brewing beer at home is a fun and easy thing that anyone can do with great success. It does require some special equipment, though. So, ask a friend who brews and brew a batch together or come by The Home Brewery in Ozark and we can help you figure out what you need. That being said, let's get on with it!!

Summer Hefeweizen

This is perfectly drinkable and quenching for your summertime thirst. This Golden beer is traditionally cloudy with yeast still in suspension. The yeast imparts a fruity flavor that blends well with the spicy character of the malted and un-malted wheat. Sorachi Ace hops bring in a unique, crisp lemon zest and lemongrass flavor that goes down clean and easy. This recipe makes about 2 to 2.5 cases of 12 oz bottles.

4 oz. malted wheat
2 oz. Belgian aromatic malt
4 oz. flaked wheat
2 oz. flaked oats
Cheesecloth bag
5 lbs. wheat dry malt extract
0.2 oz. Sorachi Ace hops (14% AA boil for 60 minutes)
0.25 oz. Sorachi Ace hops (14% AA boil for 2 minutes)
1 packet of WB 06 beer yeast (or equivalent wheat beer yeast)
3/4 c. corn sugar for priming

Note:
Cleanliness and sanitation are very important to brewing beer; be sure that you have properly cleaned and sanitized any equipment and utensils you will use.

Take the first four ingredients, the specialty grains, and tie them up in a cheesecloth bag. Fill a 16 quart stainless steel pot with about 2 gallons (8 quarts) of water. Add the grain bag to the water and slowly bring the temperature up to 170° F. Steep for 15 to 20 minutes and remove and discard the grain bag. Turn off the heat or remove the pot from the burner and stir in the wheat dry malt extract. It is a little hard to dissolve, but just keep stirring. Once it is all stirred in, bring the pot to a boil, add the first 0.2 ounce of Sorachi Ace hops and start a timer for 1 hour. These will give a little bitterness to balance the sweetness of the malt extract. You will want to watch the boil closely, as it will want to foam up and boil over. After 58 minutes, or 2 minutes before the end of the boil, add the last 0.25 ounce Sorachi Ace hops. Once the last two minutes have passed, bring the pot to the sink and surround it with ice water to help cool it down. Bring the temperature down as close to 65-70° as you can, pour it into your fermenter and top up to 5 gallons. Add the package of yeast and seal the top of the fermenter with an airlock. Once the beer has finished fermenting, stir in the priming sugar and bottle in 12 ounce re-capable bottles. Allow the bottles to sit for two weeks at room temp, chill a few and give it a try!!

Yellow Dog Pale Ale

This American Pale Ale has a distinctive bitter bite and lots of hop aroma and flavor.

4 oz. light crystal malt
2 oz. chocolate malt
Cheesecloth bag
4-3/4 lbs. light dry malt extract
1/2 lb. wheat dry malt extract
1-1/2 oz. glacier hops (6.5% AA Boil for 60 minutes)
1/2 tsp. of Irish moss (natural clarifier, boil for 15 minutes)
3/4 oz. Perle hops (4.5% AA boil for 10 minutes)
1/2 oz. Cascade hops (6% AA boil for 2 minutes)
1 packet of US-05 ale yeast
3/4 c. corn sugar

Follow the directions on the previous recipe for steeping the specialty grains and starting the 60 minute boil with the malt extract and Glacier bittering hop addition. Continue boiling for an hour adding the Irish Moss Clarifier at 15 minutes from the end of the boil (or 45 minutes after the start). Then, the addition of the Perle hops for flavor at 10 minutes from the end of the boil (or 50 minutes after the start). Finally, the addition of Cascade hops for aromatics at 2 minutes from the end of the boil (or 58 minutes after the start). Ferment and bottle as directed in the previous recipe.

Submitted by: Sheri & Todd Frye, Owners

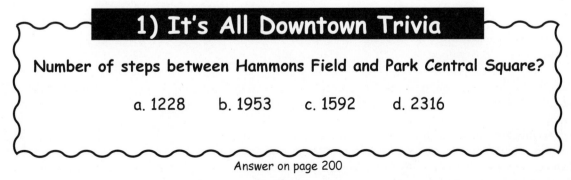

1) It's All Downtown Trivia

Number of steps between Hammons Field and Park Central Square?

a. 1228   b. 1953   c. 1592   d. 2316

Answer on page 200

Honey Heaven & the Vineyard Tea Room

2516 S Campbell
Springfield, MO 65807
417-869-0233

www.honeyheaven.com

Berry Honey Smoothie

2 c. fresh or frozen berries of choice
1 c. apple juice
1 large ripe banana
1/2 c. pecans (optional)

1 c. plain fat-free yogurt
1/4 c. Honey Heaven's Golden, Glorious & Pure Honey
1/2 c. crushed ice

Combine all ingredients in a blender. Process until smooth. Makes 3-4 servings

Just Peachy Yogurt Shake

1 - 16 oz. can peaches in juice, chilled
1 banana, peeled
2 Tbsp. Honey Heaven's Golden, Glorious & Pure Honey
Dash of cinnamon

1 c. low-fat vanilla yogurt
3 ice cubes, crushed
1/2 tsp. vanilla extract

Combine peaches with juice, vanilla yogurt, banana, ice, and honey in a blender or food processor; blend until smooth. Pour shake into chilled glasses. Sprinkle with cinnamon and serve immediately. Makes 4 cups.

Submitted by: Lena Meyer, "The Honey Lady"

Maria's Mexican Restaurant

406 South Ave,
Springfield, MO 65806
831-9339

Maria's Mexican Restaurant was one of the first businesses to help revitalize downtown Springfield. A family owned restaurant, we began in a small take-out spot on Walnut Street in 1997. Thanks to our loyal clientele we were able to move to a larger location on South Ave in 2001. We offer full service dine-in with take-out still available, a full bar with over 160 varieties of tequila. Catering available for any event.

Traditional Margarita

1-1/2 oz. premium tequila
Juice of 1 lime

3/4 oz. premium orange liqueur

Rub the rim of a 12 ounce rocks glass with a lime, dip in kosher or margarita salt, fill with ice, add ingredients and serve with lime wedge.

Monkey La La

1 oz. Vodka
4 oz. half & half

1oz. Kahlua
1/2 banana   1 c. ice

Place all ingredients in a blender & grind till a smooth consistency.

Submitted by: Monica Guest, Co-owner

The Mudhouse

323 South Ave
Springfield, MO 65806
417-832-1720

www.mudhousecoffee.com

When it comes to the way Mudhouse Coffee does business, one word says it all. "Freshness." With coffee, and enjoying a delicious cup of coffee, freshness is the only thing that really matters. What we can guarantee to our customers is that Mudhouse Coffee will be the freshest coffee available. We micro roast our coffee in small batches when we need it, so you never have to worry about our coffee sitting and losing the crucial freshness that is so important. It doesn't matter whether you purchase our coffee inside the coffeehouse or from the website; we guarantee it will be the freshest, best tasting coffee available! Open Monday-Friday 7:00am - Midnight, Saturday 7:00am - Midnight and Sunday 8:30am - 11:00pm.

Mudhouse Veggie Twist Smoothie

Several Mudhouse employees wanted a healthy, delicious smoothie with fruit and veggies in it. Hence, the Veggie Twist was created. Feeling even more adventurous? Try it with a few spinach leaves thrown in.

1 squirt honey
1 c. apricot nectar
2 frozen banana halves
1/2 c. frozen carrot chunks

Splash of pineapple juice
5-7 frozen sliced peaches
1/2 c. frozen cucumber chunks

Note:
It is very important to use frozen fruit and veggies when trying to make this smoothie thick. Using a little less juice could also add to obtaining the desired thickness. No sugar!

Pour liquids into the blender pitcher and then add the fruits and veggies. Blend until noticeably smooth and thick. You may need to tap the pitcher on the counter or stir it halfway through the blend cycle to make sure everything is blended to perfection.

Submitted by: The Mudhouse Employees

Orange Vodka Slush

1 - 6 oz. can frozen orange juice, undiluted concentrate, thawed
3/4 c. vodka
8-10 ice cubes

1 c. milk
2 Tbsp. granulated sugar

Combine orange juice concentrate, milk, vodka and sugar in container of an electric blender. Add ice cubes and blend until mixture is smooth. Makes about 5 cups.

Spiked Coffee

1-1/2 c. coffee liqueur (Kahlua)
1-1/2 c. vodka
1 orange wedge
12 ice cubes

1 c. dark creme de cacoa
1 c. espresso, cooled
Orange sugar crystals

Mix the coffee liqueur, creme de cacoa, vodka, and espresso in a small pitcher. Cover the pitcher with plastic wrap and place it in the freezer until the mixture is very cold, about 3 hours.

Meanwhile, rub the rims of 8 Martini glasses with the orange wedge. Dip the rims in the sugar crystals to coat lightly. Place the glasses in the freezer.

Add the ice cubes to the vodka mixture and briskly stir the mixture until the ice begins to melt. Strain the mixture into the prepared glasses, and serve.

Submitted by: Lori D. Cloninger, Brian Askins Mutual of Omaha Division Office

Nonna's Italian American Café

306 South Ave
Springfield, MO 65806
417-831-1222

www.nonnascafe.com

Funky, Fun, Eclectic, and Relaxed, Nonna's Italian American Café has been a downtown classic for over 12 years. Delicious Food, Homemade Desserts, Friendly Prices and a Full Bar. Featuring Full-Service Catering, Event Planning, A Jazz Guitarist Duo on Thursday Night, A Classical Guitarist on Friday Night, A Jazz Guitarist on Saturday Night, A Musical Theatre Open-Mic Sunday Night called 'The Cast Party,' Monthly Operazzi Nights, and Monthly Art Shows. Join us for the First Friday Art Walk. Open Daily. Locally World Famous.

Bellini

4 oz. prosecco   2 oz. white peach juice

Serve chilled in a champagne glass.

Nonna's Margarita

1 oz. Cuervo Gold tequila   1 oz. Amaretto di Saronno
1/2 oz. triple sec   2 oz. fresh lemonade
1/2 oz. Roses lime juice

Shake ingredients with ice. Pour over ice in a salted margarita glass. Garnish with a lime slice and a cherry.

Nonna's Lemonade

2 oz. vodka   1 oz. Grand Marnier
3 oz. fresh squeezed lemonade

Shake ingredients with ice. Pour into a chilled cocktail glass with an ice and sugared rim. Garnish with a lemon slice.

Submitted by: Martin P Almaraz, Co-owner

Parlor 88 Lounge

1111 E. Republic Rd
Springfield, MO 65807
417-882-8882

www.parlor88.com

Parlor 88 is the place to meet for cocktails and conversation. The decor is modern, and the atmosphere is decidedly trendy. The full-service bar offers an extensive martini menu along with other frozen concoctions. Sophisticated table appetizers and tempting dessert selections complete your experience at Parlor 88. Open Monday - Saturday 3:00 pm - 1:00 am. Patio and fireplace seating available.

Parlor's Party Punch

1 qt. cranberry juice
2 c. orange juice
1 pt. rainbow sherbet
1 c. champagne or sparkling wine

1 c. sugar
1 c. pineapple juice
1 c. Smirnoff Lime
2 c. 7-Up

In a large drink container, blend cranberry juice, sugar, and other fruit juices. Refrigerate until ready to serve. At serving time, stir in the rainbow sherbet and remaining ingredients.

After-Dinner Mint

1-1/2 oz. Godiva white chocolate liqueur
1/4 oz. Baileys Irish Cream
1 Oreo cookie, smashed into pea-sized chunks
1-2 c. ice (less ice yields a stronger beverage that melts more quickly)

3/4 oz. green crème de menthe liqueur
1 oz. vanilla ice cream

Garnish:

Whipped cream to taste
1/2 Oreo cookie, finely crushed

Mint leaf

Add ingredients to blender in order they are listed. Blend on the highest speed, making sure the Oreo crumbles and ice are fully blended. Serve in a tall, Pilsner-style footed glass and garnish with whipped cream, Oreo sprinkles and mint leaf. Variation: Garnish with a whole Oreo cookie as you would use a lemon slice in a fruit drink.

Submitted by: Seth Elliott, General Manager

Planet Smoothie

431 S Jefferson Ave
Suite 104
Springfield, MO 65806
417-866-2121

www.planetsmoothie.com

Planet
Smoothie®
The best tasting smoothie on the planet!

Planet Smoothie, "Your Downtown Smoothie Shop." We will gladly make you a smoothie from our delicious menu, or custom build your own to suit your taste and lifestyle! Perfect for health-nuts, kids, folks on the go, basically anyone who loves healthy, tasty smoothies! We offer a variety of discounts to Springfield college students, YMCA members and businesses. Come on by and let us make something tasty for you!

Get Your Blenders Ready!
No-Bake Oatmeal Cookie

2 oz. water
2 scoops frozen yogurt
2 oz. granola
16 oz. crushed ice

2 oz. Hershey's Chocolate Syrup
2 Tbsp. peanut butter
1 oz. oats

The Ja-Ci (jay-cee)

3 oz. water
5 oz. grape juice
1 tsp. vanilla extract

4 oz. strawberries
5 oz of acai*
9 oz. crushed ice

Bry-Man-A-Saurus

2 oz. water
2 oz. grape juice concentrate
1 tsp. vanilla extract
6 oz. crushed ice

4 oz. strawberries
1-1/2 frozen yogurt
3-1/2 oz. Acai*

*Acai can be purchased and used in these smoothies in either juice or smoothie packs from most grocery stores.

Star Candy

2 oz. water
3 oz. strawberries
1 scoop frozen yogurt
16 oz. crushed ice

3 oz. peaches
1 scoop orange sherbet
1 Tbsp. sugar or honey to sweeten

Oatmeal Shag

2 oz. water
3 oz. strawberries
2 scoops of frozen yogurt
1-1/2 Tbsp. dry milk
1 to 2 oz. oatmeal
16 oz. crushed ice

3 oz. blueberries
1/2 banana
1 tsp. vanilla
1-1/2 Tbsp. sugar
1 to 2 oz. honey

Dred-Head

4 oz. apple juice
3 oz. strawberries
2 oz. raspberries

1 Tbsp. sugar
2 oz. blueberries
24 oz. crushed ice

Submitted by: Jed Pierce, Manager & Julia Hollingsworth, Mix-master

2) It's All Downtown Trivia

Who did Wild Bill Hickok kill in the first recorded shoot-out?

a. John Campbell

b. David Tutt

c. James Robberson

d. Paul McDaniel

Answer on page 200

Rendezvous Coffee Lounge

320 Park Central West
Springfield MO 65806
417-868-0110

Rendezvous Coffee Lounge is Springfield's newest coffee shop. However, we are much more than just another coffee shop; we feature a menu with breakfast, lunch and dinner items. We are the only place in town to get a fresh brewed cup of Turkish coffee. Our pastries and cookies are fresh-baked daily, including our famous No-Bake cookies. We are in the old Randy Bacon Gallery on Park Central West. Stop by the next time you come downtown.

The Pollock

Named for Jackson Pollock, this drink was featured in Springfield's GO Magazine.

1/2 oz. tiramisu flavoring
1 oz. espresso

1/2 oz. mint flavoring
9 oz. half and half

Pull one shot of espresso (to taste) and combine with coffee flavorings in a coffee cup. Steam milk to 145°, stir well, and then combine with espresso. Top with whipped cream and a mint.

For Home:
Substitute espresso for instant espresso, or double strength coffee (our preferred).

Milk can be heated in a small pot on a stove. Be careful not to overheat! It can spoil right in front of you. Milk with lower fat can be heated to higher temperatures. All of these ingredients can be found at local grocery stores or a good coffee shop.

Submitted by: Sean and John Fleming, Owners

Trolley's Downtown Bar & Grille

107 Park Central Square
Springfield, MO 65806
417-799-0309

www.trolleysgrill.com

The three-story building that houses Trolley's Downtown Bar & Grille was purchased for the purpose of renovating the top two floors into luxury loft apartments. With that project completed, the first floor remained vacant for the next two years. After much thought over a vacant first floor, we came up with the idea of putting a restaurant in the space. Then we developed a concept for a restaurant that would fit into the extensive renovation of Downtown Springfield. Through our understanding of architecture and the public's fascination with the historical downtown buildings, a 1920's theme was conceived. The name Trolley's came from the mode of transportation that defined that era.

Watermelon Tini

1-1/2 oz. Smirnoff Watermelon
3 oz. pineapple

1/2 oz. Watermelon Pucker

Combine all ingredients in mixing tin and shake with ice. Strain and garnish with a watermelon slice.

Peanut Butter and Jelly Martini

1-1/2 oz. Frangelico

1-1/2 oz. Pama liquor

Combine all ingredients in mixing tin with ice. Shake and strain into martini glass.

Trolley's Sangria

4 oz. red wine
1/2 oz. grenadine

1 oz. orange juice
1 oz. pineapple juice

Combine all ingredients in wine glass with ice. Stir. Garnish with cherries, lemon slice, lime wedge, and an orange slice.

Submitted by: Ryan MacDonald, "The General"

The Venice at the Seville

216 E. Walnut St.
Springfield, MO 65804
417-831-2355

A MARTINI BAR & CAFÉ

Along with my beautiful wife, Jenny, and my trusting friends, Jeff and Sandy Frye, our attempt is to recreate the concept of a comfortable neighborhood gathering and of course, support our expanding families. Yet another enterprise born out of necessity. Although I've lost my edge for touting sports events, Jenny remains a genuine fashion statement who has not missed a presentation of American Idol or an issue of People Magazine; Sandy can quote Whitman, Shakespeare and others, while Jeff can discuss music, film and cultural trends. Along with a larger group of boomers and pre-Woodstock friends and associates, The Venice will attempt to hold fast to the business values of a generation too often forgotten by this 21st century. Best regards, Nick

The Alexis Martini

1-1/2 oz. raspberry vodka
1/2 oz. cranberry juice
splash roses lime juice

1/2 oz. triple sec
splash pineapple juice

Fill shaker with ice. Add Vodka, triple sec, and juices. Shake vigorously. Strain into chilled martini glass. Garnish with lime and cherry spear. Enjoy

Purple Rain Martini

2-1/2 oz. Hpnotiq
Splash of pineapple juice

Splash of pomegranate juice

Fill shaker with ice. Add Hpnotiq and juices. Shake vigorously. Strain into chilled martini glass. Garnish with cherry spear.

Submitted by: Sandy Frye, Co-owner

City of Gold Martini

1/2 oz. citrus vodka
1/2 oz. tequila
1/2 oz. triple sec
Splash of orange juice

1/2 oz. vodka
1/2 oz. rum
Splash of pineapple juice

Fill shaker with ice. Add vodkas, rum, tequila and triple sec. Shake lightly. Add juices. Strain into chilled martini glass. Garnish with lemon twist. Enjoy.

German Chocolate Cake Martini

3/4 oz. white crème de cacao
3/4 oz. Malibu rum
Drizzle of chocolate syrup

3/4 oz. dark crème de cacao
1/2 oz. cream or half and half
Shaved chocolate and or shaved coconut

Fill shaker with ice. Add crème de cacaos, Malibu and cream. Shake vigorously. Drizzle chocolate syrup into chilled martini glass. Strain into glass. Allow foam to sit on top. Garnish with chocolate shavings and or shaved coconut.

Raspberry Zinger Martini

1 oz. vodka
1 oz. cranberry juice

1 oz. raspberry liqueur or raspberry vodka
Splash of lime juice

Fill shaker with ice. Add vodka, raspberry liqueur, cranberry and lime juice. Shake lightly. Strain into chilled martini glass. Garnish with raspberries.

The Climax Martini (aka. Chocolate Covered Cherry)

1/2 oz. white creme de cacao
1/2 oz. vodka
1 oz. cream or half and half

1/2 oz. amaretto
1/2 oz. triple sec

Fill shaker with ice. Add creme de cacao, amaretto, vodka, triple sec and cream. Shake vigorously. Strain into chilled martini glass allowing foam to sit on top. Drizzle cherry juice on top or garnish with a cherry.

Submitted by: John "Coleman", Cook, Server, Bartender & Conspirator

Urban Districts Alliance

304 W. McDaniel
Springfield, MO 65806
417-831-6200

www.itsalldowntown.com

The Urban Districts Alliance (UDA) serves as an umbrella organization to coordinate and consolidate all Center City organizations into one cooperative effort. Contact Rusty Worley, UDA Executive Director or visit our website for additional information.

Kitty's Cosmo

My bartender friend, Jay, makes the best Cosmo ever! I don't know if it's the triple sec or the lime juice, all I know is that these go down way too easy.

1/2 oz. tiramisu flavoring
3 parts Vodka
Equal parts cranberry juice & lime juice

1/2 oz. mint flavoring
2 parts Triple Sec
1 lime wedge

Place a martini glass in the freezer or a bucket of ice. Pour vodka, triple sec and juices over ice and shake vigorously. Take lime wedge and run along rim of glass, leaving the lime wedge in the glass. Strain cocktail into glass and serve.

Old Fashioned Bronx Cocktail

My mom loves this drink. It was something her mom use to drink a long time ago. Now she makes it at home for special occasions and I have to admit I would sip on it whenever I got a chance.

1 oz. dry gin
1 slice orange

1 oz. French dry vermouth
1/2 slice pineapple

In a tall glass, press with spoon and smash orange slice and pineapple until juice and pulp have been blended. Add cracked ice, gin and vermouth. Shake 40 times. Strain and serve in a large cocktail glass. Garnish with orange.

Whiskey Flower

I have never been a big fan of the whiskey sour because I don't care for sour mix. This cocktail has proven to be the perfect alternative and I love the play on the name.

10 oz. bourbon
2-1/2 oz. lemon juice

1 1/4 oz. grenadine
10 oz. Perrier sparkling natural mineral water

This drink serves four so use a tall glass, about 16 to 20 ounces, and fill it half way with ice. Add grenadine, lemon juice and bourbon. Stir well. Strain 3 ounces into old fashioned glass filled with ice. Top with sparkling water.

Submitted by: Kathryn Vicat-Dlabach, Urban Districts Alliance

Appetizers

Beth's Bake Shoppe
& Tea Room

1645-D W. Republic Rd
Springfield, MO 65807
417-866-5533

www.bethsbakeshoppe.com

Beth's Bake Shoppe & Tea Room serves lunch Monday - Saturday made with delicious homemade recipes and ingredients. Our soups, quiche and specialty desserts change daily. Our fresh chicken salad has our special touch served on toasted raisin bread. Quiche has unique combinations to tempt your taste buds. Come in and check out our bakery case full of homemade cookies, bars, pies and cheesecakes. Specialty birthday, wedding and all-occasion cakes done by order only. You ruff and tuff guys don't let the tea room name scare you off. All are welcome, so come in and enjoy.

Sassy Meatballs

These meatballs are great as an appetizer or meal. I love to make these every New Years Eve.

2 lbs. of ground beef or deer
1 finely chopped yellow onion
1 Tbsp. Worcestershire sauce
Salt and pepper to taste

1 c. fine bread crumbs
1 egg, beaten
1 Tbsp. soy sauce

Sauce

12 oz. jar of chili sauce
2 Tbsp. brown sugar

1 can whole cranberries
1 tsp. lemon juice

Preheat oven to 350°. Mix first 7 ingredients together and shape into balls. Place into a large baking dish that has been sprayed with non stick spray. Cover with sauce and bake 1 hour until well browned. If you like a lot of sauce, you may double the sauce recipe.

Submitted by: Beth Perry, Owner

**Big Whiskey's American
Bar & Grill**

311 Park Central E
Springfield, MO 65806
417-862-2449

www.bigwhiskeys.com

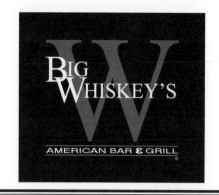

Big Whiskey's is all about starting traditions and what better time than our Happy-Hour, Monday through Friday from 4 pm - 6 pm. So come on in and enjoy some of our great half-priced appetizers and take advantage of our 2-for-1 drinks. You will be sure to enjoy our plasma TV's, NTN Trivia, our pool table or maybe some Golden Tee. While you're here, "Submit Your Toast!" Write your favorite toast on a beverage napkin and give to your server or bartender. We pick the best toast once a month. The winner gets a $50 gift card, a Big Whiskey's T-shirt and their toast displayed for a month on our website. So come on in and start a new tradition. Traditions starting daily…

Buffalo Dip

16 oz. softened cream cheese
1-1/2 c. Franks Red Hot sauce

5 chicken breasts, shredded
3 c. white cheese, shredded

Spread softened cream cheese evenly in the bottom of 12 x 9 inch baking pan. Mix shredded chicken and hot sauce in a bowl. Spread mixture on top of the cream cheese. Sprinkle shredded cheese over the top. Cover with foil and bake at 350° for 10 minutes. Once out of the oven, mix the dip together thoroughly and serve.

Big W's Chicken Nachos

10 oz. tortilla chips
3 oz. cooked chicken, diced
3 oz. taco sauce or salsa
2 oz. tomatoes, diced
2 oz. jalapeno, sliced

2 oz. refried beans
6 oz. cheddar cheese, shredded
3 oz. lettuce, shredded
3 oz. sour cream

Pre-heat oven to 375°. Spread chips out evenly on a 12 x 9 inch baking sheet. Drizzle refried beans over chips. Then spread chicken over chips and top with shredded cheddar cheese. Toast in oven at 375° for 5-7 minutes. Remove from oven. Pour taco sauce over the top of nachos. Next, add the shredded lettuce and diced tomatoes and jalapenos. Finish with desired amount of sour cream and serve.

Submitted by: Joshua Hite, Chef

Cassils Cafes Inc.

2925 W. Republic Rd.
Springfield, MO 65807
417-851-1104

2601 N. Cresthaven
Springfield, MO 65803
417-866-2221

www.cassils.com

Cassils is your neighborhood gathering place. Whether it's stopping by on the way to work for a latte and fresh cinnamon roll, taking a client to lunch, studying for finals on your laptop, having dinner with your family, or enjoying live entertainment with your friends, Cassils is your place.

At Cassils, we started by bringing to Springfield some of the best coffees the world has to offer, roasted and blended by some of the best roasters in the country. We added to that our award-winning menu of unique, casual appetizers, entrees, baked goodies, and desserts. We serve it all up in a comfortable, friendly atmosphere you're going to love.

Football Season Guacamole with Bruschetta Chips

4 avocados
1/4 c. onion
5 Tbsp. olive oil
Salt and pepper to taste

1 c. "citrus" juice
1/4 c. cilantro
1/2 c. half & half

Peel the avocados, chop up the onion, and chop up the cilantro. Place in a blender the olive oil, half & half, and your choice of fresh citrus juices (we recommend lime and lemon). Add the avocados (don't forget to remove the big 'ol seeds), the onion, and cilantro. Add salt and pepper to taste. Blend until smooth.

Bruschetta Chips:
1 baguette
Dried basil

Olive oil
Directions

Slice the baguette diagonally into thin slices, approximately 1/4 inch or less thick. Lightly brush the top of each slice with olive oil. Sprinkle each slice with basil. Grill the slices on a griddle or in a skillet until golden brown. Serve with the guacamole, other dips, or just eat 'em by themselves.

Submitted by: Kevin Cassil, Country-boy, Scientist, & Restaurant Owner

Clary's Restaurant

900 E Battlefield Rd
Springfield, MO 65804
417-866-6200

www.eatatclarys.com

The relationship between Farmer, Fisherman and Chef coupled with the evolution of rapid airfreight, has revolutionized the restaurant industry, particularly among fine dining restaurants. At Clary's we now buy produce, poultry, and meat directly from local farmers. We order fish directly from the West coast, Hawaii, and the Gulf of Mexico, and it is flown overnight from the location to your table. We get produce flown to us overnight the day it is picked in California. Our menu now changes regularly to reflect the products we are getting in daily! Our philosophy has not changed, that is, to provide you with the most exciting dining experience possible.

Szechwan Shrimp

5 large shrimp, peeled and de-veined, tails on
1 Tbsp. dark sesame oil
1 tsp. garlic, minced
1/4 c. soy sauce

1/2 c. flour
1/2 tsp. red pepper flakes
1 tsp. fresh ginger, minced
1/4 c. rice wine vinegar

In a bowl, toss shrimp with flour and shake off excess flour. Get a small skillet very hot. Add sesame oil, shrimp, garlic, red pepper, and ginger and sauté until shrimp is just done, about 1 minute per side. Remove shrimp from pan and set aside in a warm place. Add soy sauce and rice vinegar to pan and bring to a boil. Simmer until sauce begins to thicken, Pour over warm shrimp.

Submitted by: James Clary, Owner & Executive Chef

Fire & Ice Restaurant and Bar

At Oasis Hotel and Convention Center
2546 N. Glenstone
Springfield, MO 65803
417-522-7711

www.oasisfireandice.com

The Oasis Hotel proudly presents Fire & Ice Restaurant & Bar, where an exquisite atmosphere and culinary creativity welcome hotel guests and the general public. Fire & Ice features Springfield's only curved counter-top ice bar, and offers seating that extends to the indoor pool and its surrounding fountains and plant life, as well as seasonal seating around the hotel's outdoor pool. The open-plan kitchen allows patrons to watch a show of flames behind the ice bar performed by Executive Chef Wing Yee Leong and his team as they prepare the evening's entrees. Dinner fare at Fire & Ice includes seafood delights, steak specialties, and a variety of beef, shrimp, and chicken dishes showcasing Chef Wing's mastery of the wok.

Whiskey Pepper Glazed Sirloin on Crostini with Caramelized Onion & Boursin Cheese Crumbles

2 - 8 oz. top sirloin, tri-tip or culottes cut beef
1 baguette, sliced (1/4 inch slices, "French Cut")
1 Tbsp. chopped garlic

1/2 yellow onion
1/4 c. extra virgin olive oil
6 oz. Boursin cheese

To Make Paste:
4 Tbsp. roasted garlic flavor paste
8 Tbsp. Worcestershire sauce

4 Tbsp. tri-pepper flakes (red, black, & green)

To Make Whiskey Pepper Glaze:
1 Tbsp. tri-pepper flakes
1 Tbsp. chopped garlic
1 c. pineapple juice
2 c. brown sugar
1/2 c. balsamic vinaigrette

1 Tbsp. onion powder
1 Tbsp. hot sauce
1/2 c. whiskey
2 Tbsp. beef base

Prepare a paste by combining garlic flavor paste, tri-pepper flakes and Worcestershire sauce. Rub paste generously onto steaks then charbroil or broil to desired doneness. Prepare glaze by combining ingredients in a saucepan. Bring to a boil, reduce heat and simmer for 15 minutes. Finish steaks by glazing with sauce, but save some glaze for finishing the crostinis.

Put 1/4 cup olive oil in saucepan; add 1 Tbsp. chopped garlic and sweat garlic at medium heat for 20 minutes. Slice the baguette into 1/4 inch slices on the bias (oblong). Brush with garlic olive oil and toast crostini baguette in 350° oven for

7-10 minutes. Julienne 1/2 yellow onion into 1/8 inch half-moon pieces (across the width of the onion). Sauté onion in skillet until caramelization stage for 10-15 minutes over medium to high heat. Reserve and cool.

After broiling and glazing the steaks, let the steaks rest for 15 minutes. After resting, slice the steaks across the grain into 1/2 inch x 2 inch 1/4 inch thick slices. Place the steak slices on the garlic crostini. Top with the caramelized onion and Boursin cheese crumbles. Drizzle remaining whiskey pepper glaze over each completely built crostini.

Submitted by: Wing Yee Leong, Executive Chef

Fedora Social House

On The Square Downtown
300 Park Central East
Springfield, MO 65806
417-832-9514

www.fedoradowntown.com

When it's time to decompress from the day's events, you do have lots of choices in Springfield. If you're looking for urbane and polished, yet comfortable and unhurried, Fedora Social House is your easy answer to the evening. Is your office in the downtown area? Come share one of our delicious cheese fondues with friends from work. Look no further than Fedora Social House for a unique venue to host your private party or corporate function. You'll make a great impression on friends and associates with an extensive spread of desserts, fondues, and more!

Fondue Siciliano

1 oz. of your favorite marinara sauce
3 oz. mozzarella or any Italian blend
Pinch of garlic sauce and Italian seasoning

Add ingredients together in your fondue pot. The beauty of fondue dippers is that you can use whatever you want. It's a good way to clean out your crisper and use all of those random vegetables.

Submitted by: Drex Holt, Manager

Galloway Station
Bar & Grill

4211 S. Lone Pine Ave
Springfield Mo 65804
417-881-9730

myspace.com/gallowaystation

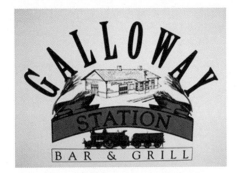

Hidden in the middle of southwest Springfield and part of historic Galloway Village, Galloway Station has Springfield's best outdoor dining patio. The view is relaxed and calming. The Galloway Trail and its walkers, joggers, and bikers etc. are always passing by traveling from Sequiota Park. You can also see the railroad tracks as the building itself is an old historic train station. The decor and charm of the building still keeps true to its heritage. With a tasty menu, cold beer, and live music on the weekends, you really can't go wrong with Galloway Station.

Veggie Ciabatta

4 fresh Portobello mushrooms, washed
1 Tbsp. olive oil
1 tsp. salt

1 Tbsp. red wine vinegar
1 tsp. fresh ground pepper

Dip an uncooked Portobello mushroom in vinegar and oil, then sprinkle with salt and pepper and bake for 15 minutes.

Loaf ciabatta bread
2 Tbsp. olive oil
1 red pepper, sliced
1 red onion, sliced

1/2 c. cream cheese
1 green pepper, sliced
1 tomato, sliced
4 slices Swiss cheese

While the mushrooms are baking, slice ciabatta bread 5 to 6 inches long, then cut in half and brush exterior with olive oil. Spread cream cheese inside and bake for 5 minutes. In a small pan add one tablespoon of olive oil with green and red peppers; sauté for 3 to 4 minutes. On the prepped Portobello mushroom, place sautéed peppers, two tomato slices, one slice red onion and one slice Swiss cheese. Melt cheese on veggies in the oven or on the grill for about 6 minutes. Serves 4-6 people.

Submitted by: John Tsahiridis, Manager

Gem of India
Restaurant & Bar

211 W. Battlefield
Springfield, MO 65807
417-881-9558

www.gemofindia.net

Gem of India has been serving Springfield with fine Indian cuisine for many years. The chef/owner has worked in fine Indian restaurants in Boston since 1992. We serve authentic Indian cuisine made with the finest and freshest ingredients. We strive to provide excellent service and mouth-watering delicacies with an enticing ambience. We hope to serve Springfield for a long time to come.

Lamb Roganjosh

1 c. lamb, minced
1 tsp. garam masala
3 tomatoes, skinned and chopped
Big pinch of saffron, soaked in lukewarm milk
4 Tbsp. olive oil
1 Tbsp. coriander seeds powder (Dhania powder)
6 red chiles
6 garlic cloves

2 medium sized onions, sliced
4 green chiles, chopped
1 c. fresh curd, beaten
15 cashews
1 inch long piece of ginger
1 Tbsp. turmeric
1 Tbsp. cumin seed

First grind ginger, coriander seeds, turmeric powder, red chiles, cumin seeds, and garlic with adequate quantity of salt to a thick paste. Now heat oil. Fry onions, green chiles, and tomatoes till brown and oil begins to separate. Add masala paste and simmer for 3 minutes. Add minced lamb meat. Add beaten curd and a cup of water. Cook till meat is tender and gravy is thick. Add garam masala, soaked saffron and cashews. Cover it with a lid for a few minutes. Serve hot, garnished with chopped coriander leaves.

Submitted by: Singh Gurdev, Owner

Maria's Mexican Restaurant

406 South Ave,
Springfield, MO 65806
831-9339

Maria's Mexican Restaurant was one of the first businesses to help revitalize downtown Springfield. A family owned restaurant, we began in a small take-out spot on Walnut Street in 1997. Thanks to our loyal clientele we were able to move to a larger location on South Ave in 2001. We offer full service dine-in with take-out still available, a full bar with over 160 varieties of tequila. Catering available for any event.

Shrimp Ceviche

1 lb. medium shrimp, peeled & deveined
1/2 c. fresh lime juice
1 fresh jalapeno, finely chopped
1/3 c. chopped cilantro

2 qts. water
1 c. red onion, finely chopped
4 medium size ripe tomatoes, diced

Bring water to a boil, add shrimp and cook 2 minutes. Remove shrimp from pan and place on a sheet tray to cool. Once cooled, cut shrimp in half and place in a bowl; add lime juice, onions and jalapeno and mix. Cover; set in refrigerator for at least 1 hour or up to 24 hours. Add tomatoes and cilantro to shrimp mixture and refrigerate for 1/2 hour. Serve with corn tortilla chips.

Submitted by: Monica Guest, Co-owner

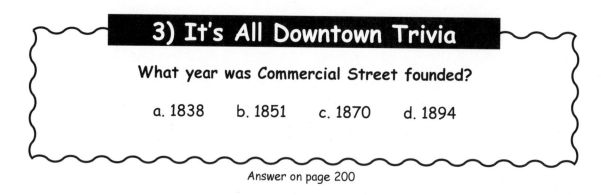

3) It's All Downtown Trivia

What year was Commercial Street founded?

a. 1838   b. 1851   c. 1870   d. 1894

Answer on page 200

Metro Builders Supply

3252 N Glenstone
Springfield MO 65803
417-833-1113

www.metrobuilderssupply.com

METRO BUILDERS SUPPLY
"Your Home Appliance Specialist"

Metro Builders Supply is the largest appliance distributor in the Midwest. With nine stores in four states, Metro has the buying power to offer the lowest possible price on more than 30 brands of major appliances. Whether you are a builder, contractor, or homeowner, Metro has the product to meet your needs and your budget. Each of our locations provides an extensive display of products, many showcased in kitchen cabinetry. Our employee-owned company prides itself with expert salespeople who offer years of appliance sales experience and extraordinary customer service. Our showroom in Springfield, MO offers an extensive lighting department as well. The largest selection, the lowest prices... experience Metro!

Asian Pear & Cheese Crostini

A favorite recipe from the live kitchen at Metro Builders Supply.

16 slices, 3/8 inch (baguette style French bread)
1 sm. ripe Asian pear, cored and sliced very thin
Fresh mint sprigs (optional)

4 oz. Gorgonzola cheese or other blue cheese, crumbled
2 Tbsp. honey

Place bread slices on a large baking sheet. Broil 4-5 inches from heat for 30-60 seconds or until bread is toasted. Turn slices over; top bread slices with Gorgonzola cheese. Broil for 30-60 seconds until cheese is bubbly and bread is toasted. Top bread slices with pear slices. Lightly drizzle pear slices with honey. Arrange on serving platter. If desired, garnish with mint sprigs. Yield: 16 servings.

Submitted By: Judy Bilyeu, Metro Builders Supply

Metropolitan Grill

2931 East Battlefield
Springfield, MO 65804
417-889-4951

www.metropolitan-grill.com

Metropolitan Grill is the "Cheers" of fine dining. Where Spain meets Italy in the heart of the Ozarks. I love people, and I love to cook, so the restaurant is my vehicle to achieve what I love. Relax and let the atmosphere and a great glass of wine fill your senses while we create unique dishes for you in our display kitchen.

My Cooking Philosophy: 'Creation.' As an Executive Chef I challenge my kitchen staff every day to 'create, not copy'. Many artists can paint Picasso; many pianists can play Mozart; and yes, many Chefs can make Emeril's dishes. My menu is inspired by my restaurant family and my emotions. Enjoy our "creations."

Portobello Appetizer

Home-made beef stock
3 c. water
1 tsp. crushed red pepper
1 Tbsp. unsalted butter
1 tsp. minced garlic

Cornstarch
6 medium Portobello mushrooms, thinly sliced
1/4 c. soy sauce
1/2 c. red wine

Home-made beef stock:
Bring 1 cup beef broth (brand of your choice) and 1/4 cup red wine to a boil. Mix 3 cups cold tap water and 1/2 cup cornstarch; whisk together. Add more cornstarch, if necessary, until you have a slightly thick paste. Set aside.

Portobello appetizer:
Add butter, soy sauce, garlic and crushed red pepper in a 10 inch sauté pan. Sauté until butter is completely melted and all ingredients are mixed. Add Portobello's. Sauté together until all mushrooms are coated with pan mixture. De-glaze with remaining red wine, and let mushrooms cook down. Finally, toss with 4 ounces of beef stock.

Submitted by: Pat Duran, Owner & Executive Chef

Mille's Turn of the Century Café

313 S Jefferson Ave
Springfield, MO 65806
(417) 831-1996

www.millescafe.com

August of 1999, Mille's Turn of The Century Café opened on Jefferson in Historic Downtown Springfield. An Urban Casual Café, Mille's brought unique, yet affordable dining to downtown.

Open for lunch and dinner, Mille's truly has something for everyone. With over 100 items on the menu, a full bar and wine list, four private dining/meeting rooms, outside seating and a 225 person Banquet room that is perfect for weddings, class reunions or a surprise get together.

Roasted Red Pepper Hummus with Warm Pita

1 - 20 oz. can garbanzo beans
1 Tbsp. sesame oil
1 tsp. lemon juice
1/2 c. pimento, drained
6-8 pitas, warmed and cut into quarters

1/2 c. olive oil
1 Tbsp. cumin
1 tsp. garlic, minced
Salt and pepper to taste

Drain garbanzo beans and place into a food processor. Add all remaining ingredients, except pita, and puree until desired consistency. It can be very smooth or semi chunky, whatever your taste. Remove from food processor and place in bowl. Serve with warm pita and enjoy!!

Submitted by: Mark Giacin, Mille's Turn of the Century Café

Nonna's Italian American Café

306 South Ave
Springfield, MO 65806
417-831-1222

www.nonnascafe.com

Funky, Fun, Eclectic, and Relaxed, Nonna's Italian American Café has been a downtown classic for over 12 years. Delicious Food, Homemade Desserts, Friendly Prices and a Full Bar. Featuring Full-Service Catering, Event Planning, A Jazz Guitarist Duo on Thursday Night, A Classical Guitarist on Friday Night, A Jazz Guitarist on Saturday Night, A Musical Theatre Open-Mic Sunday Night called 'The Cast Party,' Monthly Operazzi Nights, and Monthly Art Shows. Join us for the First Friday Art Walk. Open Daily. Locally World Famous.

Artichoke Bruschetta Served With Crostini

Crostini:

1 baguette
1 c. parmesan cheese, grated

2 cloves of garlic, crushed
Olive oil

Preheat oven to 400°. Slice baguette into 1/4 inch thick slices about 3 inches long.
Lightly brush baguettes with olive oil, and spread a small amount of garlic on each piece.
Lightly sprinkle each slice with parmesan cheese and place in the oven for 10 minutes
or until golden brown. Let cool and set aside.

Bruschetta:

4 tomatoes, diced small (no seeds)
1 clove of garlic, crushed
4 artichoke hearts in brine, roughly chopped
3 Tbsp. balsamic vinegar

1 medium red onion, diced small
2 Tbsp. fresh basil, chopped
2 Tbsp. extra virgin olive oil
Salt and white pepper to taste

Combine in a mixing bowl, tomatoes, red onion, garlic, artichoke hearts and basil. Mix in the olive oil and then the balsamic vinegar. Season with salt and white pepper to taste,
and serve a small amount on each of the crostini.

Submitted by: Martin P Almaraz, Co-owner

Pappy's Place Cafe

943 N. Main Avenue
Springfield, MO 65802
417-866-8744

Pappy's Place has stood at this location since 1904. While now housing a bar/restaurant, the store first began as a family-owned shoe repair shop. Shortly after that, the owners opened a grocery store and kept it that way until the 1920s. New owners opened a cafe on the property in 1924. Following Prohibition, the cafe applied for a beer-by-the-drink license. This license, which is still held by Pappy's, is the oldest continuous license in Springfield. Pappy's Place may be old, and not very well-known, but it is a place of character. The people are friendly, the food is good and the beer is cold. A casual atmosphere makes for a laid-back time. For many people, it is a place of good memories.

Moroccan Rolls

Pappy's is a musician friendly restaurant. At almost any time of any day, there will be at least one local or traveling musician. A guitar player from "the Bay" area gave this dish its name.

1 boiled potato, mashed
1 onion, chopped
1 Tbsp. ground cumin
Hot pepper flake

1 lb. ground beef
1 Tbsp. curry powder
Egg roll wrappers
Salt and pepper

Brown ground beef in skillet. Drain and add onions. Cook for about 5 minutes. Season with curry, cumin, hot pepper flakes, salt and pepper. Add the mashed potato and stir until it is incorporated into the seasoned beef. Arrange egg roll wrapper with a corner facing you. Spoon mixture into the center (a little below center). Roll like an egg roll. Take the bottom corner and fold over mixture. Moisten all edges of the wrapper with water; fold left and right corners into center, then roll away from you. Fry Moroccan Rolls until golden brown.

Submitted by: Jack Rauhoff, Chef

Parlor 88 Lounge

1111 E. Republic Rd
Springfield, MO 65807
417-882-8882

www.parlor88.com

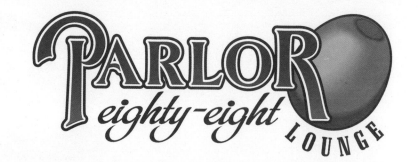

Parlor 88 is the place to meet for cocktails and conversation. The decor is modern, and the atmosphere is decidedly trendy. The full-service bar offers an extensive martini menu along with other frozen concoctions. Sophisticated table appetizers and tempting dessert selections complete your experience at Parlor 88. Open Monday - Saturday 3:00 pm - 1:00 am. Patio and fireplace seating available.

Cucumber Dip

3 lbs. cream cheese
2 cucumbers, diced
2 tsp. celery salt
1 tsp. salt

1/4 tub sour cream
1/2 c. dill
1 tsp. pepper

Dice cucumbers and put in strainer; coat top of cucumbers with table salt. Toss cucumbers well and allow to drip water into a pan until water is extracted (about 1/2 hour). Mix all ingredients in a mixing bowl.

Submitted by: Seth Elliott, General Manager

4) It's All Downtown Trivia

Number of brick pavers on Patton Alley?
a. 37,940   b. 43,652   c. 48,185   d. 53,928

Answer on page 200

Patton Alley Pub

313 S Patton Ave
Springfield, MO 65806
417-865-1188

www.pattonalleypub.com

Patton Alley Pub is Springfield's downtown place to hang out with friends, listen to live music and have a great meal! With over 40 beers on tap, it's the place to be downtown! Patton Alley Pub was voted Best Bar, Best Bar Food, Best Happy Hour and Best Beer Menu by 417 Magazine readers. If you would like to know more, please contact us, and we'll give you more information so that your event can be delicious as well as perfect! We have great bands every Friday and Saturday night, for a complete list please go to www.myspace.com/pattonalleypub.

Fried Green Tomatoes

1/2 c. all-purpose flour (you can season it with salt and pepper if you like)
1 c. cornmeal
3 to 4 green tomatoes, sliced
Egg wash (1 egg and 1 cup milk whisked together)
Vegetable oil, for frying

When your oil is hot, dip the tomato slices first in the flour, then the egg wash and finally the cornmeal, and once again in the egg wash and cornmeal. Place tomatoes in the oil; fry them until golden brown, turning once. Season with salt and pepper and serve them with apple butter.

Submitted by: Eric Zackrison, Chef

Peabody's

312 E. Commercial St
Springfield, Mo. 65803
417-832-8585

Beer Battered Portabello Mushrooms

2 large Portobello mushroom caps, cut into 1/4 inch strips
1 c. all purpose flour
1/2 tsp. garlic powder

1 c. wheat beer (room temperature)
1/2 tsp. seasoned salt
1/2 tsp. onion powder

Mix dry ingredients and beer until smooth. Dredge clean, dry Portobello strips in batter.
Deep fry at 325°, turning once until golden brown (about 1-1/2 minutes on each side).
Place in a circular pattern with a cup of ranch dressing in the middle of the plate.

Submitted by: Dorana Delmer, Head Chef

Peabody's Stuffed Portabello Mushrooms

4-6 portabella mushrooms
1 – 8 oz. pkg. cream cheese
1 tsp. onion powder
1 c. shredded cheddar cheese

1 lb. breakfast sausage
4-5 green onions, chopped
1 tsp. garlic powder
Seasoned bread crumbs to taste

Clean mushrooms and remove stems. Chop stems finely and set aside. Brown sausage and drain. Mix rest of the ingredients with cooked sausage and chopped stems. Brush the mushroom caps with olive oil. Stuff mushrooms with the sausage mixture. Placed stuffed mushrooms on jelly-roll pan or a pan with sides. Sprinkle mushrooms with seasoned bread crumbs and additional shredded cheddar cheese. Bake in a 350° oven for 15 minutes or until cheese has melted and mushrooms are hot.

Submitted by: Ron Peabody, Owner

Soups

Andy's Frozen Custard

Springfield
2119 N. Glenstone
3147 E. Sunshine
2726 S. Campbell Ave.
4420 S. Campbell Ave.

Branson
3415 W. Hwy 76

888-60-ANDYS

www.eatandys.com

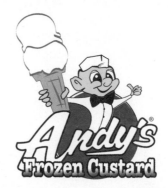

Andy's has made a science out of frozen custard. We've perfected the method for preparing and serving custard in its highest form, giving you an unparalleled frozen treat. We use the finest ingredients in our mix, a secret recipe of milk, cream, sugar and eggs, which is processed and shipped to Andy's stores within 24 hours to maintain ultimate freshness. Our proprietary frozen custard machines (less than ten are manufactured each year) are customized to Andy's exacting specifications. Andy's Frozen Custard is made fresh hourly and only served at its peak flavor potential of sixty minutes to ensure that our customers get the best frozen custard each time they visit. It's just part of the Andy's difference.

Sopa de Tortilla

1/2 green pepper, minced
1 medium onion, minced
2 cloves garlic, minced
14-1/2 oz. can tomatoes
1-1/2 c. beef broth
10-3/4 oz. can tomato soup
1 tsp. ground cumin
1 tsp. salt or to taste
2 tsp. Worcestershire sauce
1/2 c. grated cheddar or Monterey Jack cheese

3 ribs celery, minced
1 jalapeno pepper, minced
2 Tbsp. oil
5 oz. Rotel tomatoes and green chilies (1/2 can)
3-1/2 c. chicken broth
2 c. water
1 tsp. chili powder
1/2 tsp. lemon pepper seasoning
6 corn tortillas cut in 1-inch squares

Sauté the first 5 ingredients in oil in a large kettle until soft, but not brown. Add remaining ingredients, except tortillas and cheese, and simmer for 50 minutes. Add tortillas and cook 10 minutes. Pour into mugs and sprinkle with cheese. Ladle soup into bowls and let your guests help themselves to chopped tomatoes, chopped ripe olives, chopped scallions, sour cream, cheese or toasted tortilla triangles. Yield: 6-8 servings.

Submitted by: Dana & Andy Kuntz, Owners

Bambu Vietnamese Cuisine

1338 E. Battlefield
Springfield, MO 65804
417-881-9881

www.springfieldbambu.com

Bambu is a family Vietnamese restaurant which aims to enrich the lives of its community, family and friends with delicious, fresh and richly infused traditional dishes. All the stocks here are made on the premises and simmered over twelve hours to produce a marvelous depth of flavor. We encourage you to play with your food and to slurp your soup! We'll kindly provide bibs upon request because it's hard not to get the soup spattered all over you. Enjoy your meal!

Beef Noodle Soup (pho bo)

Makes 8 satisfying (American-sized) bowls

For the broth:
2 medium yellow onions (about 1 lb. total)
5-6 lbs. beef soup bones (marrow and knuckle bones)
6 whole cloves
1-1/2 Tbsp. salt
4-inch piece ginger (about 4 oz.)
5 star anise (40 star points total)
3-inch cinnamon stick
4 Tbsp. fish sauce
1 oz. (1 inch chunk) yellow rock sugar (duong phen; see Note)
1 lb. piece of beef chuck, rump, brisket or cross rib roast, cut into 2 x 4 inch pieces (weight after trimming)

For the bowls:
1-1/2 to 2 lb. small (1/8 inch wide) dried or fresh banh pho noodles ("rice sticks" or Thai chantaboon)
1/2 lb. raw eye of round, sirloin, London broil or tri-tip steak, thinly sliced across the grain (1/16 inch thick; freeze for 15 min. to make it easier to slice)
1 medium yellow onion, sliced paper-thin, left to soak for 30 min. in a bowl of cold water
3 or 4 scallions, green part only, cut into thin rings
1/3 c. cilantro, chopped (ngo)
Ground black pepper

Optional garnishes arranged on a plate and placed at the table:
Sprigs of spearmint (hung lui) and Asian/Thai basil (hung que)
Leaves of thorny cilantro (ngo gai)
Bean sprouts (about 1/2 lb.)
Red hot chiles (such as Thai bird or dragon), thinly sliced
Lime wedges

Prepare the broth:

Char onion and ginger. Use an open flame on grill or gas stove. Place onions and ginger on cooking grate and let skin burn. (If using stove, turn on exhaust fan and open a window.) After about 15 minutes, they will soften and become sweetly fragrant. Use tongs to occasionally rotate them and to grab and discard any flyaway onion skin. You do not have to blacken entire surface, just enough to slightly cook onion and ginger.

Let cool. Under warm water, remove charred onion skin; trim and discard blackened parts of root or stem ends. If ginger skin is puckered and blistered, smash ginger with flat side of knife to loosen flesh from skin. Otherwise, use sharp paring knife to remove skin, running ginger under warm water to wash off blackened bits. Set aside.

Parboil bones. Place bones in stockpot (minimum 12 quart capacity) and cover with cold water. Over high heat, bring to boil. Boil vigorously 2-3 minutes to allow impurities to be released. Dump bones and water into sink and rinse bones with warm water. Quickly scrub stockpot to remove any residue. Return bones to pot.

Simmer broth. Add 6 quarts water to pot; bring to boil over high heat, then lower flame to gently simmer. Use ladle to skim any scum that rises to surface. Add remaining broth ingredients and cook 1-1/2 hours. Boneless meat should be slightly chewy but not tough. When it is cooked to your liking, remove it and place in bowl of cold water for 10 minutes; this prevents the meat from drying up and turning dark as it cools. Drain the meat; cool, then refrigerate. Allow broth to continue cooking; in total, the broth should simmer 3 hours. Strain broth through fine strainer. If desired, remove any bits of gelatinous tendon from bones to add to your bowl. Store tendon with cooked beef. Discard solids. Use ladle to skim as much fat from top of broth as you like. (Cool it and refrigerate it overnight to make this task easier; reheat before continuing.) Taste and adjust flavor with additional salt, fish sauce and yellow rock sugar. The broth should taste slightly too strong because the noodles and other ingredients are not salted. (If you've gone too far, add water to dilute.) Makes about 4 quarts.

Assemble bowls. The key is to be organized and have everything ready to go. Thinly slice cooked meat. For best results, make sure it's cold.

Heat broth and ready noodles. To ensure good timing, reheat broth over medium flame as you're assembling bowls. If you're using dried noodles, cover with hot tap water and soak 15-20 minutes, until softened and opaque white. Drain in colander. For fresh rice noodles, just untangle and briefly rinse in a colander with cold water.

Blanch noodles. Fill 3 or 4 quart saucepan with water and bring to boil. For each bowl, use long-handle strainer to blanch a portion of noodles. As soon as noodles have collapsed and lost their stiffness (10-20 seconds), pull strainer from water, letting water drain back into saucepan. Empty noodles into bowls. Noodles should occupy 1/4 to 1/3 of bowl; the latter is for noodle lovers, while the former is for those who prize broth. If desired, after blanching noodles, blanch bean sprouts for 30 seconds in same saucepan. They should slightly wilt but retain some crunch. Drain and add to the garnish plate.

continued on page 55

Add other ingredients. Place slices of cooked meat, raw meat and tendon (if using) atop noodles. (If your cooked meat is not at room temperature, blanch slices for few seconds in hot water from above.) Garnish with onion, scallion and chopped cilantro. Finish with black pepper.

Ladle in broth and serve. Bring broth to rolling boil. Check seasoning. Ladle broth into each bowl, distributing hot liquid evenly so as to cook raw beef and warm other ingredients. Serve with garnish plate.

Note:
Yellow rock sugar (a.k.a. lump sugar) is sold in one-pound boxes at Chinese and Southeast Asian markets.
Break up large chunks with hammer.

Variations:
If you want to replicate the splendorous options available at pho shops, head to the butcher counter at a Vietnamese or Chinese market. There you'll find white cords of gan (beef tendon) and thin pieces of nam (outside flank, not flank steak). While tendon requires no preparation prior to cooking, nam should be rolled and tied with string for easy handling. Simmer it and the beef tendon in the cooking broth for two hours, or until chewy-tender. Airy book tripe (sach) is already cooked when you buy it. Before using, wash and gently squeeze it dry. Slice it thinly to make fringe-like pieces to be added to the bowl during assembly. For beef meatballs (bo vien), purchase them in Asian markets in the refrigerator case; they are already precooked. Slice each one in half and drop into broth to heat through. When you're ready to serve, ladle them out with the broth to top each bowl.

Submitted by: Thuy "Twee" Dam, Owner

5) It's All Downtown Trivia

What is the tallest building (above sea level) in Missouri?
a. Hawthorn Park   b. Hammons Tower
c. Gateway Arch (630 feet)   d. One Kansas City Place (632 feet)

Answer on page 200

**Big Momma's Coffee
& Espresso Bar**

217 E Commercial St
Springfield, MO 65803
417-865-9911

www.bigmommascoffee.com

You have to get up very early to get the first cup of coffee at Big Momma's Coffee House and Espresso Bar in Springfield. Located on the often overlooked Commercial Street Historic district, owner Lyle Foster; a Chicago native, was initially interested in refurbishing a building into loft apartments. Then he had an epiphany. "I believe in the notion of a 3rd place. Everybody has a job, a home, and they need a third place to hang out. And that should be a coffee shop." With that in mind, Big Momma's was born.

You never know who you'll run into at Big Momma's. From students and business people to city leaders and artists -- people stream in day and night. The walls feature works from local photographers and artists. Momma's Back Porch hosts dinner theater regularly and live jazz on Tuesdays.

Roasted Garlic Bean Soup

2 whole garlic bulbs
1 pint heavy cream
1/2 onion, finely chopped
2 to 3 Tbsp. olive oil

3 cans vegetable or chicken broth
3 cans white beans such as Navy, Cannelini or Great Northern
1/2 tsp. sage
Salt and pepper to taste

Remove outer papery skin from garlic. Pour a dash of olive oil over each bulb. Wrap loosely in foil and roast in 450° oven for about 45 minutes. Sauté onion in 1 tablespoon olive oil until translucent. Half way through sauté, add sage to onions. In large stockpot, pour beans and stock. Add onion mixture. When cool to the touch, push softened roasted garlic out of skins and into food processor. Pulse for about thirty seconds with 1-2 tablespoons olive oil. Spoon mixture into soup. Stir to blend. Add cream, salt and pepper. Simmer low for 20-30 minutes, stirring occasionally. Serve with crusty bread.

Submitted by: Joe Terry, Barista and Baker

BRUNO'S RESTAURANT
Fine Italian Casual Dining

Bruno Gargiulo brings the tastes of his Italian home to Springfield, Missouri. He is making authentic Italian cuisine with the best ingredients he can find. His specialty is Southern Italian cooking. Gargiulo makes almost everything on-site. He spends each morning preparing dough for their bread and pizza crusts. "Everything is special on the menu because you won't find it anywhere else." More than 60 Italian wines representing different regions of Italy are offered at Bruno's.

Zuppa Di Ceci (chickpea soup)

2 Tbsp. butter
1-1/2 c. dried chickpeas (or 2-1/2 c. canned chickpeas)
2 oz. onion, chopped
1 oz. carrots, chopped
4 Tbsp. extra virgin olive oil

4 garlic cloves, crushed
1 tsp. paprika
1 oz. celery, chopped
1 oz. mushrooms, chopped
Salt and pepper to taste

Soak the chickpeas overnight in salted water. Cook the chickpeas in their brine in a medium saucepan until tender. Drain and set aside. In a saucepan, melt the butter. Add the garlic and sauté until lightly golden. Add the onion, carrot, celery, and mushrooms; sauté until tender. Add two cups of chickpeas, paprika and enough water to cover the mixture. Bring to a boil and simmer for five minutes. Transfer the mixture to a food processor or blender and puree, adding the olive oil in a slow steady stream. Adjust the salt and pepper to taste and return to the pan to warm until serving. Deep fry the remaining chickpeas until golden and crisp. Place the soup in bowls and garnish with a drizzle of olive oil and the fried chickpeas. Serves 4.

Submitted by: Bruno Gargiulo, Owner

Clary's Restaurant

900 E Battlefield Rd
Springfield, MO 65804
417-866-6200

www.eatatclarys.com

The relationship between Farmer, Fisherman and Chef coupled with the evolution of rapid airfreight, has revolutionized the restaurant industry, particularly among fine dining restaurants. At Clary's we now buy produce, poultry, and meat directly from local farmers. We order fish directly from the West coast, Hawaii, and the Gulf of Mexico, and it is flown overnight from the location to your table. We get produce flown to us overnight the day it is picked in California. Our menu now changes regularly to reflect the products we are getting in daily! Our philosophy has not changed, that is, to provide you with the most exciting dining experience possible.

Curried Butternut Squash Soup

1 squash
3 Tbsp. shallot
2 Tbsp. olive oil
1 Tbsp. salt and pepper mix

1 1/2 c. chicken stock
2 tsp. curry powder
3/4 c. cream

Pre-heat oven to 350°. Cut squash in half lengthwise. Brush inside of squash with olive oil and place inside down on cookie sheet. Roast for about 1 hour 15 minutes until squash feels soft when pressed from the outside. Set aside to cool.

Sauté the shallots in olive oil in hot pan until translucent. Reduce heat and add chicken stock and cream. With a large spoon, remove seeds from squash and scoop pulp from skin. In a food processor or food mill, process squash until very smooth. Add squash to cream mixture. Add a little more stock if too thick. Adjust seasonings with salt and pepper and slowly bring to a boil. Remove from heat and strain through a very fine strainer (chinois), twice. Serve hot.

Submitted by: James Clary, Owner & Executive C

Cooks Kettle Restaurant

At Victory Trade School
200 W. Commercial
Springfield, MO 65803
417-864-2210

www.victorytradeschool.org

Named for Everett and Esther Cook, founders of Springfield Victory Mission, the Cook's Kettle Restaurant provides the culinary laboratory setting for VTS. This restaurant, newly remodeled with a "French Bistro" look, has 2 classically French trained chefs instructing the students as they attend classes in Victory Trade School and receive hands-on training while working various positions in the restaurant. The customers of Cook's Kettle Restaurant agree they return because of the high quality of the food, the low prices, and the cleanliness of the facility. This economical place to eat is a model of how a restaurant can serve good food and practice good hygiene and sanitation. This "student-operated" restaurant provides variety in the menu and all customers are served with professionalism.

Chili Formula

1 Tbsp. oil to brown the meat
1 c. small onion, diced
14-1/2 oz. can beef broth
14-1/2 oz. can tomato sauce
1 to 2 cans beans (black beans, pinto beans, kidney, or other) use two cans if you like plenty of beans or leave them out if you want.
1/2 tsp. salt
1 Tbsp. corn starch and 1 Tbsp. water to make slurry

2 lbs. meat (coarse ground beef, regular ground beef, ground turkey, ground pork, or ground venison) use any of these or a combination of them.
14-1/2 oz. can tomatoes, diced
1 tsp. chili powder
2 tsp. cumin powder
2 tsp. sugar
1 Tbsp. fresh garlic puree

Ground meat method:
Brown meat in a heavy bottom pot that is preheated; put the onion in with the meat as it browns. Drain off all the fat and discard. Now add all of the ingredients to the pot except for the slurry. Simmer for 10-15 minutes on low; then thicken with the slurry.

Diced steak version:
Small dice 2 pounds of any kind of shoulder steak, round steak, or roast of beef. The less expensive cuts work great for this. Brown the meat in a heavy bottom pot and add the onions to sweat for a couple of minutes. Next, add 2 cups of water and the canned beef broth; simmer the meat until it is all the way soft. Now add all the rest of the ingredients except the slurry and simmer 10 minutes more; then thicken with the slurry.

Submitted by: Chadwick M Isom, Executive Chef

Downtown Springfield Association

304 W McDaniel St
Springfield, MO 65806
417-831-6200

www.itsalldowntown.com

"Serving the heart of the city by improving and promoting the diverse historic, cultural, social and economic environment of downtown Springfield." Formed in 1965, DSA is a volunteer-driven membership-based organization funded by member participation and events. Its mission includes business development and projects to draw new customers and business prospects to downtown. The DSA also works with other downtown organizations in a collaborative effort to support and promote business downtown. Major DSA programs include downtown capital and infrastructure improvement prioritization and implementation, networking socials, and major retail events such as Sidewalk sales, holiday open houses and the Downtown Discount Card program.

Tom's Manhattan Clam Chowder

My dad loves clam chowder and as a Brooklyn boy, his favorite has always been Manhattan Style. He loves it so much that he went so far as to ask for it in Boston, to which the waitress replied, "If you eat Manhattan Clam Chowder in Boston, you pee sitting down." It took me awhile to put together a recipe my dad really likes and this one is his favorite.

4 - 7-1/2 oz. cans of clams drained (save the juice)	5 slices of bacon, diced
1 - 16 oz. can of tomato purée	2 c. potato, diced
1 c. celery, diced	1 c. onion, diced
1 c. water	2 c. chicken stock
1-1/2 tsp. salt	Dash of hot sauce (optional)
2 Tbsp. cold water	2 Tbsp. flour
Italian seasoning to taste	

In a large Dutch oven partially cook bacon; add celery and onion. Sauté until soft. Add the clam juice and all other ingredients, except clams, water and flour. Cover and simmer about 20 minutes or until the potatoes are tender.

Blend the flour with the cold water adding a little of the hot broth to make a paste. Return flour/water mixture to the chowder, stirring until blended. Bring to a boil and simmer for 5 to 8 minutes. Add the clams and Italian season to taste. Heat through and serve.

Submitted by: Kathryn Vicat-Dlabach, UDA Community Development & Festival Assistant

Easy's Cajun Restaurant & Bar

1710 S Glenstone Ave
Springfield, MO 65804
417-881-3939

www.easysrestaurant.com

If you could turn the colorful trademarks of Mardi Gras into an edible dish, then you might find yourself at Easy's Cajun Restaurant & Bar with its soothing colors, relaxing tables and creative menu items. This family-owned and operated eatery serves each freshly prepared meal with lots of passion. Nothing but the finest ingredients go into the Southern recipes, and although they may be Asian, their hearty comfort food is very much known to be as good or better than some of the restaurants down South. With plenty of entrees and original fusion items, each dish is served hot and fresh with a side of soul..

Jambalaya

3 lbs. chicken breast, 1-inch cubes
1/2 c. cooking oil
1 bunch green onions, finely chopped (separate greens from whites)
4 celery stalks, finely chopped
5 tsp. black pepper
3 tsp. salt, or to taste
9 c. fresh chicken broth

2 lbs. Andoulle sausage, sliced
2 tsp. sugar
5 large onions, finely chopped
1 large bell pepper, finely chopped
3 tsp. hot sauce
4-1/2 c. long grain rice

Brown sausage in cooking oil in 12 quart iron pot, about 10 minutes on medium heat. Remove and set aside. Brown chicken in left-over oil until cooked, but not burnt. Add sausage and cook on medium heat uncovered until golden brown, about 20 minutes. Add chopped onions, celery, and bell pepper. Cook until dark brown and wilted. Add 9 cups of broth and all seasonings: add more seasoning and salt if desired. Bring to a good boil, spoon off excess oil if desired. Add raw rice and stir until water becomes opaque and thick: stir gently not to break rice. Cover with tight lid and simmer on low for 20-30 minutes, or until rice is cooked (do not open lid unless you are sure it is done, your jambalaya will lose moisture if you do). Gently fluff rice and add green onion tops. Do not stir again. Cover and let sit 15 minutes and then serve. A black cast iron pot makes the best jambalaya.

Submitted by: Kevin Kwok, Executive Chef & Owner

First Friday Art Walk

411 N. Sherman Parkway
Springfield, Missouri 65802
417-849-8255

www.ffaw.org

First Friday Art Walk, held 6-10 p.m. the first Friday of each month, is a free walking tour of downtown Springfield's 20-plus art galleries. The event features works by local, regional and national artists, as well as live demonstrations and performances, all in support of First Friday Art Walk's nonprofit mission of promoting fine art and economic vitality in the Downtown Arts District. For more information, give us a call or visit our website.

Farmer's Market Zucchini Soup

2 Tbsp. unsalted butter
1-2 celery stalks, sliced
2 tsp. fresh thyme leaves, chopped
2 tsp. sea salt
6 c. chicken stock or low-sodium canned chicken broth

1-2 med. carrots, sliced
1 sm. onion, sliced
5 med. zucchini, trimmed, cut in half length wise, and sliced (about 7-1/2 cups)

In an 8-quart soup pot, melt the butter over medium heat. Add the carrots, celery and onion, and sauté for 10 minutes, stirring occasionally. Add the thyme, zucchini and stock; increase the heat to high and bring to a boil. Reduce the heat to medium and simmer for 10 minutes or until the zucchini are tender. Stir in the salt.

Working in batches, puree the soup in a blender or food processor until smooth. Serve the soup chilled in the summer or warm in the winter. Garnish with olive-oil croutons. Serves 6-8.

Tip:
For a quick, elegant first course for eight, sauté 8 large sea scallops until just done (about 2 minutes on each side). Place a sea scallop in the middle of each bowl of chilled zucchini soup.

Submitted by: Kylee Allen, Hawthorn Galleries

Gallery Bistro

Gallery Bistro

221 E Walnut St
Springfield, MO 65806
417-866-0555

www.gallerybistrodowntown.com

Gallery
Bistro

Gallery Bistro is located on Historic Walnut Street in Downtown Springfield; just two doors down from the Landers Theatre and next to the Vandivort Theatre. Our contemporary cuisine is an eclectic mix of Asian, French, English, Spanish and Down-home.

Friendly, attentive and knowledgeable service is our trademark. Combined with our extensive wine collection and massive martini repertoire, our patrons are ensured of a fabulous dining experience. Gallery Bistro is the place to go for dinner or light fare before the show, or after the curtain falls. Late night cocktails and an appetizer - or our famous mushroom sage soup - are favorites of Springfield theater-goers.

Gazpacho

This is a great summer soup. It's easy to make, healthy and uses everyday Missouri garden vegetables.

1 lb. 10 oz. ripe tomatoes, roughly chopped & deseeded
2 Tbsp. red wine vinegar
1 red onion, chopped
1 green pepper, deseeded and chopped
Salt and freshly ground black pepper

1/2 pt. tomato juice
1 Tbsp. olive oil, pinch sugar, few drops Tabasco (optional)
1/2 cucumber, chopped
Large bunch fresh basil, torn
Ice cubes to serve

Place half of the tomatoes into a food processor or blender along with the tomato juice, vinegar, oil, sugar and Tabasco. Blend until smooth; if the mixture is a little thick, then add a little more tomato juice. Stir through the remaining ingredients, add a few ice cubes and serve.

Submitted by: Peter Tinson, Owner & Executive Chef

Gem of India
Restaurant & Bar

211 W. Battlefield
Springfield, MO 65807
417-881-9558

www.gemofindia.net

Gem of India has been serving Springfield with fine Indian cuisine for many years. The chef/owner has worked in fine Indian restaurants in Boston since 1992. We serve authentic Indian cuisine made with the finest and freshest ingredients. We strive to provide excellent service and mouth-watering delicacies with an enticing ambience. We hope to serve Springfield for a long time to come.

Indian Chicken Soup

3-1/2 oz. boneless chicken, shredded
1 Tbsp. garlic, finely chopped
1 Tbsp. white flour
1 Tbsp. oil
1 Tbsp. fresh cream

2 c. chicken stock
1 tsp. cumin seeds
2 tsp. butter
Salt & white pepper to taste

Heat the butter in a pan and fry the shredded chicken pieces till tender. Remove and set aside. In a pan heat oil and let the cumin seeds splutter. Add the chopped garlic and sauté for a few seconds. Add the white flour and fry for 1 minute. Add the chicken, chicken stock, white pepper powder and salt. Cook on medium level for about 4 minutes while stirring all the time. Stir in the fresh cream just before serving.

Note:
For 2 cups of chicken stock, cook about 1 pound of chicken bones with one 4-1/2 cups of water; add chopped onions and garlic till the stock is reduced to half the quantity.

Submitted by: Singh Gurdev, Owner

Honey Heaven & the Vineyard Tea Room

2516 S Campbell
Springfield, MO 65807
417-869-0233

www.honeyheaven.com

A Honey of a Pumpkin Soup

2 Tbsp. butter
2 celery stalks, chopped
6 c. pumpkin, peeled, seeded, chopped
5 whole cloves
2 Tbsp. Honey Heaven's Golden, Glorious & Pure Honey

2 large carrots, chopped
1 large onion, chopped
6 c. or more of chicken stock or canned broth
1/2 c. whipping cream

Melt butter over medium-high heat. Add carrots, celery, and onion; sauté until tender, about 8 minutes. Add pumpkin and 6 cups stock. Cover and simmer until pumpkin is very tender, about 25 minutes. Puree soup in batches in blender. Return to pan. Stir in cream and honey. Bring to simmer. Season to taste with salt and pepper. (Can be made one day ahead. Chill. Bring to simmer before serving, thinning with more stock if desired.) Serves 4-6.

Submitted by: Lena Meyer, "The Honey Lady"

J. Bucks Restaurant

2825 S. Glenstone Ave.
Springfield, MO 65804
417-823-7167

www.jbucks.com

A genuine American restaurant with a great bar. That's the concept behind J. Bucks Restaurant. Created out of our belief in great food, fantastic service and a fun, casual atmosphere, we're perfect for just about any occasion or gathering. Established in 1999 and named after Joe, Jack, and Julie Buck, the legendary broadcasting family. Our vision of the classic American restaurant celebrates the rich history and tradition of excellence the Buck family is known for. We're proud to help carry on their legacy for all to enjoy.

Tomato & Gorgonzola Soup

1- #10 can tomatoes, crushed
2 lg. yellow onions, diced
1/4 c. dried oregano
4 Tbsp. butter

1- #10 can tomatoes, diced
1/2 gal. of chicken stock
6 c. gorgonzola cheese
Salt & pepper to taste

Sauté onions in butter for 3-4 min. or until golden and translucent. Add crushed and diced tomatoes and chicken stock to pot and bring to a simmer. Add oregano, salt and pepper. Simmer for 15-20 minutes. Remove pot from heat and add gorgonzola cheese. These ingredients yield a very large pot of soup but is very good stored in the refrigerator. You will need to add desired portion of gorgonzola cheese if you make in smaller quantities.

Submitted by: Steve Thompson, Executive Chef

6) It's All Downtown Trivia

What is the number of attendees each year on Walnut Street during Arts-fest and Cider Days?

a. 20,000   b. 30,000   c. 40,000   d. 60,000

Answer on page 200

Mutual of Omaha

Brian Askins Division Office
1435 E Bradford Pkwy, Suite 105
Springfield, MO 65804
417-863-7250

brian.askins@mutualofomaha.com

What are your dreams? At Mutual of Omaha-Springfield, our professional representatives can help you create a plan to reach your financial dreams with a complete line of insurance and financial products including; Life Insurance, Disability Income insurance, Annuities, Medicare Supplement insurance, and Long-Term Care insurance. Just like you, we care about our community, we support the Urban Districts Alliance-Taste of Springfield Cookbook and the dreams they want to reach for our community. Contact us today to start planning how to reach your dreams.

California Chicken Soup

1 c. water
2 c. cooked, cubed chicken
1/2 c. carrots, sliced
1/2 to 3/4 tsp. crushed oregano
1 tsp. Lawry's lemon pepper
1-9 oz. pkg. frozen cut broccoli, thawed

3 14-1/2 oz. cans chicken broth
1 small onion, chopped
1/2 tsp. Lawry's garlic powder with parsley
1 bay leaf
4 oz. cheese tortellini or shell pasta

In large stockpot, combine all ingredients except tortellini and broccoli. Bring to a boil. Add tortellini. Reduce heat to low and cook, uncovered for 20 minutes. Add broccoli cooking 10 minutes longer. Serve Hot. Meal idea: serve with cheddar biscuits. Makes 4 to 6 servings.

Hint:
1 pound bag of assorted frozen vegetables can replace onion, carrots and broccoli.

Submitted by: Diana Wardlaw, Brian Askins Mutual of Omaha Division Office

Peabody's

312 E. Commercial St
Springfield, Mo. 65803
417-832-8585

COME FOR THE FOOD, STAY FOR THE FUN

The idea behind Peabody's Restaurant grew from the countless family and friends we have entertained in our home. Many have enjoyed Ron's cooking and encouraged him to begin his own restaurant. We hope you get pleasure from the unique charm Peabody's provides while enjoying some of our favorite dishes. These dishes are inspired from Ron's travels throughout the world during his twenty-year career in the United States Navy. Our family has loved them, and we know you will too!

Tomato Basil with White Beans

2 celery stalks, finely chopped
1 tsp. fresh minced garlic

1/2 purple onion, finely chopped

Sauté above ingredients until translucent. Add the following ingredients to the sautéed celery, onion, and garlic.

2 c. chicken stock or broth
6 oz. can tomato paste
2 - 12 oz. cans white beans (rinsed and drained)

4 - 8 oz. cans tomatoes with liquid, diced
1/8 c. dried basil (dried works better than fresh in this recipe)

Bring to a boil, lower heat and simmer 30 minutes. Garnish serving with a dollop of sour cream.

Submitted by: Dorana Delmer, Head Chef

Rodizio Brazilian Grill

3371 E Montclair St
Springfield, MO 65804
417-881-8882

www.springfieldrodizio.com

Whether an intimate dinner for two, an employee lunch for 10 or a business meeting and meal for 50, our Brazilian Steak House is the perfect place. Our fixed-price menu includes Brazilian Cheese bread and appetizers, the cold bar, and all 18 selections of beef, pork, lamb and poultry. You enjoy as much as you want and when you want it - with our unique Rodizio-style service. Our elegant yet fun atmosphere along with private and customized dining areas will accommodate almost any need. We are proud to share with you our food, traditions and culture ~ all in a beautiful setting. We invite you to explore our web site and learn more about our authentic Churrascaria (shoo-rah-scah-REE-ah) style of dining.

Cream of Morel Mushrooms

3 oz. Morel mushrooms, sliced
2 tsp. parsley, chopped
Salt and pepper to taste
2 tsp. butter

1/4 c. onion, chopped
2 c. vegetable stock
1 c. of heavy cream

Melt butter in a pan and add the mushrooms. Cook for 2 minutes on low heat, stirring constantly. Add the onion and vegetable stock and proceed to cook for 25 minutes. Add salt and pepper and garnish with parsley. Let simmer for 30 minutes.

Submitted by: Angel Kim, Executive Chef

7) It's All Downtown Trivia

Elvis Presley performed in or visited all the following Springfield venues, except:

a. Shrine Mosque

b. Gillioz Theatre

c. Hammons Student Center

d. Ozark Mountain Jubilee

Answer on page 200

Tuscan Grill

3631 E Sunshine St
Springfield, MO 65809
(417) 883-7800

www.parrinobros.com

Jay Parrino moved here from St. Louis in 1983, the year that he opened J. Parrinos' Pasta House and Bar on East Battlefield. Having been in the restaurant business here in Springfield since then, he has opened and operated different restaurants in the local market. In addition to the J. Parrinos locations in the Galleria on Battlefield and in the Heer's Building, Jay was also co-founder of the Pasta Express chain of carry-out pasta locations that have been operating since 1991. He has since sold all other concepts except Pasta Pronto on National. While most of the restaurants have had an Italian flavor to the cuisine, steaks and seafood are not out of his realm, or catering to large groups. His newest adventure is The Tuscan Grill, where besides Italian food; there are plenty of steak and chicken options to choose from.

Homemade Shrimp Soup

A friend had a recipe for a Fish Casserole that needed shrimp soup; I couldn't find any in the grocery stores so I made my own. Good for topping baked or fried fish.

1 qt. half and half
3 stalks celery, chopped (1 cup)
1/2 c. butter, melted
3/4 c. flour

1 c. chicken stock
1/4 c. onion, chopped
1 Tbsp. Cajun spice
16 rough cut 31-40 shrimp

Add celery, onion and butter to pot; sauté until onion is translucent and flavorful. Add flour, stirring constantly until roux is formed; turn down heat to simmer and continue cooking, until flour is toasted lightly. Add Cajun spice; when incorporated well, add half and half, stirring constantly. Add chicken stock. Adjust seasoning; add shrimp, stirring until shrimp are cooked thru. Makes about 6 servings.

Submitted by: Jay Parrino, Owner & Chef

Taste of Springfield

Salads

Andy's Frozen Custard

Springfield
2119 N. Glenstone
3147 E. Sunshine
2726 S. Campbell Ave.
4420 S. Campbell Ave.

Branson
3415 W. Hwy 76

888-60-ANDYS

www.eatandys.com

Andy's has made a science out of frozen custard. We've perfected the method for preparing and serving custard in its highest form, giving you an unparalleled frozen treat. We use the finest ingredients in our mix, a secret recipe of milk, cream, sugar and eggs, which is processed and shipped to Andy's stores within 24 hours to maintain ultimate freshness. Our proprietary frozen custard machines (less than ten are manufactured each year) are customized to Andy's exacting specifications. Andy's Frozen Custard is made fresh hourly and only served at its peak flavor potential of sixty minutes to ensure that our customers get the best frozen custard each time they visit. It's just part of the Andy's difference.

Apple Salad

4-6 apples, chopped
1 small can pineapple pieces
1 c. pecan pieces

2-3 c. seedless grapes, cut in half
1/4 lb. mini marshmallows
1 c. raisins (optional)

Dressing:
Blend pineapple juice, Miracle Whip, and sugar to taste. Mix with fruit and nuts.

Broccoli & Cauliflower Salad

1 head cauliflower, diced
1 red pepper, diced

1 bunch broccoli, diced
1 red or green onion, diced

Dressing:
1 c. Miracle Whip
1/3 c. vinegar
2 tsp. mustard

1/2 c. sugar
1/2 c. oil
Salt & pepper

Mix well; pour dressing over vegetables. Make a day ahead and store in refrigerator.

Submitted by: Carol Kuntz, Vice President, Founder and Andy's Mom

Bambu Vietnamese Cuisine

1338 E. Battlefield
Springfield, MO 65804
417-881-9881

www.springfieldbambu.com

Bambu is a family Vietnamese restaurant which aims to enrich the lives of its community, family and friends with delicious, fresh and richly infused traditional dishes. All the stocks here are made on the premises and simmered over twelve hours to produce a marvelous depth of flavor. We encourage you to play with your food and to slurp your soup! We'll kindly provide bibs upon request because it's hard not to get the soup spattered all over you. Enjoy your meal!

Hue Chicken Salad (ga bop)

The two most critical ingredients in this recipe are the chicken, which must be juicy and cooked just right, and the rau ram, which must be used liberally. In Hue, the ancient imperial capital of Vietnam where this dish originated, ga bop is served as a snack with beer or as a side to chao ga (chicken rice soup). To me it's delicious served any way, even with just a bowl of steamed rice! This technique for cooking the chicken is based on the Chinese method of submerging a whole bird in boiling water. This simple method produces moist, succulent chicken every single time.

1/2 whole chicken, thigh and leg scored for faster cooking
1 tsp. black peppercorns, lightly toasted in a pan and ground, or 1/2 tsp. ground black pepper
1 tsp. kosher salt or to taste
2 tsp. sugar
2-1/2 Tbsp. freshly squeezed lime juice
1 small yellow onion, sliced paper-thin, rinsed (about 1/2 c.)
2 Thai bird chilies or 1 Serrano chili, chopped or to taste (optional)
1 c. loosely packed rau ram leaves or mint leaves
1/2 Tbsp. vegetable oil
4 butter lettuce leaves, preferably inner leaves

Fill a pot with 2 quarts water and bring to vigorous boil. Add the chicken and bring it back to another boil. Reduce the heat and simmer 10 minutes. Turn off the heat and let the chicken sit in the pot, covered, for 20 minutes. Remove the chicken and set it aside to cool. Remove and discard the skin and bones from the chicken. Hand shred the meat into 1/4 inch thick strips and transfer to a mixing bowl. Add the black pepper, salt and sugar and gently massage into the chicken. Add the lime juice, onions, chilies, rau ram and oil and toss gently. To serve, line a serving plate with the butter lettuce and place the chicken on top. Serves 4.

Submitted by: Thuy "Twee" Dam, Owner

Big Whiskey's American Bar & Grill

311 Park Central E
Springfield, MO 65806
417-862-2449

www.bigwhiskeys.com

Big Whiskey's is all about starting traditions and what better time than our Happy-Hour, Monday through Friday from 4 pm - 6 pm. So come on in and enjoy some of our great half-priced appetizers and take advantage of our 2-for-1 drinks. You will be sure to enjoy our plasma TV's, NTN Trivia, our pool table or maybe some Golden Tee. While you're here, "Submit Your Toast!" Write your favorite toast on a beverage napkin and give to your server or bartender. We pick the best toast once a month. The winner gets a $50 gift card, a Big Whiskey's T-shirt and their toast displayed for a month on our website. So come on in and start a new tradition. Traditions starting daily…

Big W's Turkey Ranch Salad

3 oz. turkey, diced
2 oz. tomatoes, diced
2 oz. cheddar cheese, shredded
2 oz. ranch dressing

7 oz. lettuce, shredded
2 oz. cucumbers, sliced
2 oz. bacon bits

Place all ingredients in a mixing bowl. Mix together and pour into a salad bowl. Top with diced tomatoes and serve.

Submitted by: Joshua Hite, Chef

Curried Chicken Salad

1 pkg. chicken salad (Sam's Club carries good brand)
1 c. dried cranberries
1/4 c. curry powder
2 tsp. pepper

1/2 c. almonds, sliced
1 bundle green onion, diced
2 tsp. salt
Served with lettuce

Mix all ingredients in a mixing bowl, add almonds and dried cranberries after all other ingredients are fully incorporated.

Submitted by: Seth Elliott, General Manager - Parlor 88 Lounge

Bruno's Ristorante

416 South Ave
Springfield, MO 65806
417-866-0007

www.brunos-restaurant.net

BRUNO'S RESTAURANT
Fine Italian Casual Dining

Bruno Gargiulo brings the tastes of his Italian home to Springfield, Missouri. He is making authentic Italian cuisine with the best ingredients he can find. His specialty is Southern Italian cooking. Gargiulo makes almost everything on-site. He spends each morning preparing dough for their bread and pizza crusts. "Everything is special on the menu because you won't find it anywhere else." More than 60 Italian wines representing different regions of Italy are offered at Bruno's.

Insalata Di Verdure Alla Griglia (salad of grilled vegetables)

Marinade:
1/4 c. white wine vinegar
1 tsp. dry basil
3 garlic cloves, crushed

1-1/2 c. extra virgin olive oil
1 tsp. dry oregano
Pinch of black pepper

Vegetables:
1 eggplant
2 yellow squash
1 red bell pepper
20 - 1/3 oz. Ciliegine mozzarella balls

2 zucchini
1 large Portobello mushroom
1/2 lb. mixed greens

Combine the marinade ingredients in a large bowl and whisk together. Slice the vegetables lengthwise, so there are 8 pieces of each. Toss the vegetables in the marinade, and let stand for at least 30 minutes. Remove from the marinade, shaking off the excess, and grill until tender. Divide the greens between four plates and arrange the vegetables on top with the mozzarella. Serves 4.

Submitted by: Bruno Gargiulo, Owner

Clary's Restaurant

900 E Battlefield Rd
Springfield, MO 65804
417-866-6200

www.eatatclarys.com

The relationship between Farmer, Fisherman and Chef coupled with the evolution of rapid airfreight, has revolutionized the restaurant industry, particularly among fine dining restaurants. At Clary's we now buy produce, poultry, and meat directly from local farmers. We order fish directly from the West coast, Hawaii, and the Gulf of Mexico, and it is flown overnight from the location to your table. We get produce flown to us overnight the day it is picked in California. Our menu now changes regularly to reflect the products we are getting in daily! Our philosophy has not changed, that is, to provide you with the most exciting dining experience possible.

Chopped Salad

1/4 c. feta cheese
1/4 c. pine nuts, toasted
1 oz. balsamic dressing

1/4 c. dried cherries
2 c. red leaf lettuce, shredded
Salt and pepper to taste

Mix all ingredients in large wooden or metal bowl. Serve immediately.

Dilled Chicken Salad

2 lbs. boneless chicken, steamed and cubed
1/2 c. black olives, diced
1/2 c. chopped pecans

3/4 c. celery, finely diced
1/2 c. green onion

For the dressing:
1/2 c. mayonnaise
1 Tbsp. dill
Salt and pepper to taste

1/2 c. sour cream
2 Tbsp. lemon juice

Submitted by: James Clary, Owner & Executive Chef

Gallery Bistro

Gallery Bistro is located on Historic Walnut Street in Downtown Springfield; just two doors down from the Landers Theatre and next to the Vandivort Theatre. Our contemporary cuisine is an eclectic mix of Asian, French, English, Spanish and Down-home.

Friendly, attentive and knowledgeable service is our trademark. Combined with our extensive wine collection and massive martini repertoire, our patrons are ensured of a fabulous dining experience. Gallery Bistro is the place to go for dinner or light fare before the show, or after the curtain falls. Late night cocktails and an appetizer - or our famous mushroom sage soup - are favorites of Springfield theater-goers.

Crisp Salmon Salad

12 oz. new potatoes, cooked and sliced
1/2 c. mixed salad leaves
1 Tbsp. coarse ground black pepper
1 Tbsp. whole-grain mustard

8 cherry tomatoes, halved
2 pieces skinless salmon fillet, each weighing approx 3.5 oz.
Grated rind and juice of 1 orange

Toss together the potato slices and tomatoes and divide between 2 serving dishes. Pile the salad leaves on top. Press one side of each salmon fillet into the pepper. Heat a non-stick frying pan or a griddle until hot, place the salmon in and cook for 3-4 minutes each side until just cooked. Lay the salmon on top of the salad leaves, mix together the orange rind and juice and the mustard; drizzle over the salad and serve.

Submitted by: Peter Tinson, Owner & Executive Chef

Honey Heaven & the Vineyard Tea Room

2516 S Campbell
Springfield, MO 65807
417-869-0233

www.honeyheaven.com

Honey Harvest Fruit Salad

1/2 c. Honey Heaven's Golden, Glorious & Pure Honey   2 Tbsp. lime juice
1 qt. sliced fruit (a colorful combination of apples, pears, grapes, melons & berries)
1/3 c. nuts of choice

Blend honey and lime juice. Toss fruit, nuts & honey-lime dressing all together and chill until ready to serve.

Zesty Summer Salad with Spicy Lime Dressing

1 c. fresh lime juice
1 small onion, cut in half
1 small red pepper, cut in half
1 head Romaine lettuce, torn in pieces
6 oz. marinated artichoke hearts, drained
8-12 black olives
1 small yellow squash

1/2 c. Honey Heaven's Golden, Glorious & Pure Honey
1 garlic clove
4 sprigs fresh parsley
1 avocado, peeled and sliced
1 ripe tomato
1 Tbsp. olive oil

Spicy Lime Dressing:
To make the dressing, combine in a blender the lime juice, honey, onion, garlic, olive oil and red pepper. Process until all ingredients are pureed. Add sprigs of parsley and blend for a second more. Chill until ready to use.

Tomato Salad:
Place romaine lettuce leaves on each of four individual salad plates. Add the avocado, marinated artichoke pieces, and tomato. Sprinkle lightly with dressing and garnish with olives.

Submitted by: Lena Meyer, "The Honey Lady"

J. Bucks Restaurant

2825 S. Glenstone Ave.
Springfield, MO 65804
417-823-7167

www.jbucks.com

A genuine American restaurant with a great bar. That's the concept behind J. Bucks. Created out of our belief in great food, fantastic service and a fun, casual atmosphere, we're perfect for just about any occasion or gathering. Established in 1999 and named after Joe, Jack, and Julie Buck, the legendary broadcasting family. Our vision of the classic American restaurant celebrates the rich history and tradition of excellence the Buck family is known for. We're proud to help carry on their legacy for all to enjoy.

Club Salad

4 oz. chicken tenders, fried
1/4 c. hard boiled eggs, diced
1/4 c. parmesan cheese, shredded
2 oz. honey Dijon salad dressing

5 oz. mixed greens
1/4 c. cooked bacon, chopped
1/2 c. croutons

Mix greens and honey Dijon together in a large mixing bowl. Cook and dice chicken tenders. Top salad with hard boiled eggs and bacon. Add cooked chicken tenders. Top with croutons and parmesan cheese.

Submitted by: Chef Thompson

8) It's All Downtown Trivia

Which transportation route didn't come through downtown Springfield?

a. Trail of Tears

b. Butterfield Stage Line

c. Route 66

d. All of the above

Answer on page 200

Metro Builders Supply

3252 N Glenstone
Springfield MO 65803
417-833-1113

www.metrobuilderssupply.com

METRO BUILDERS SUPPLY
"Your Home Appliance Specialist"

Metro Builders Supply is the largest appliance distributor in the Midwest. With nine stores in four states, Metro has the buying power to offer the lowest possible price on more than 30 brands of major appliances. Whether you are a builder, contractor, or homeowner, Metro has the product to meet your needs and your budget. Each of our locations provides an extensive display of products, many showcased in kitchen cabinetry. Our employee-owned company prides itself with expert salespeople who offer years of appliance sales experience and extraordinary customer service. Our showroom in Springfield, MO offers an extensive lighting department as well. The largest selection, the lowest prices... experience Metro!

Bistro Chicken Pasta Salad

A delicious salad first featured in the Metro Experience Cookbook at Metro Builders Supply.

2 lbs. cooked penne pasta
1 c. cherry tomatoes, quartered
1/2 c. Italian salad dressing, powdered mix
1/4 c. red onion, chopped

2 boneless, skinless chicken breasts, halved
1 - 4 oz. pkg. feta cheese, crumbled
1/3 c. fresh basil leaves, lightly packed & cut into strips
1/4 c. sun dried tomatoes (not oil packed)

Grill or broil chicken breasts and cut into 1/4 inch slices. Toss all ingredients except chicken. Top pasta mixture with chicken. Serve warm or chilled.

Submitted By: Judy Bilyeu, Metro Builders Supply

Mille's Turn of the Century Café

313 S Jefferson Ave
Springfield, MO 65806
(417) 831-1996

www.millescafe.com

August of 1999, Mille's Turn of The Century Café opened on Jefferson in Historic Downtown Springfield. An Urban Casual Café, Mille's brought unique, yet affordable dining to downtown.

Open for lunch and dinner, Mille's truly has something for everyone. With over 100 items on the menu, a full bar and wine list, four private dining/meeting rooms, outside seating and a 225 person Banquet room that is perfect for weddings, class reunions or a surprise get together.

Blackened Steak Salad

4-5 oz. mixed greens
2-3 Tbsp. feta cheese
12 grapes, halved
3 oz. balsamic vinaigrette

4 mushrooms, sliced
1/4 c. walnut pieces
5 oz. steak, sliced
1 tsp. blackening seasoning

Place lettuce greens, feta, walnuts, mushrooms and vinaigrette in a mixing bowl and toss well. Place salad in a serving dish. Take slices of steak and warm in a sauté pan with blackening seasoning till warm. Place on top of salad mixture. Serve with some hot crusty bread and enjoy!

Submitted by: Matt Marquart, Mille's Turn of the Century Cafe

9) It's All Downtown Trivia

Ronald and Nancy Reagan dedicated which film at the Gillioz in 1952?

a. The Stratton Story

b. The Luckiest Man

c. The Winning Team

d. Win one for the Gipper

Answer on page 200

Ocean Zen Pacific Rim

600 E Battlefield St
Springfield, MO 65807
417-889-9596

www.eatoceanzen.com

Springfield's premiere Pacific Rim restaurant, Ocean Zen has brought the fusion of East meets west to the Ozarks. Featuring many culinary delights including sushi. The Tan Brothers (John and Chef Johnson Tan) opened in November of 2004. In the spring of 2007 they expanded to a larger building located at 600 East Battlefield. Saving the atmosphere people have grown to love, the new building offers a larger bar area, three banquet rooms to accommodate larger parties and dining. Open for lunch seven days a week from 11am-3pm. Dinners start at 4:30pm to close. Ocean Zen offers a drive thru, as well as catering options.

Fresh Heirloom Tomato Carpaccio Salad
with Shaved Prosciutto and Fresh Buffalo Mozzarella

1 ea. heirloom tomato, sliced thin
2 oz. shaved thin prosciutto
1 oz. tear drop tomatoes
2 oz. olive oil

3 oz. fresh buffalo mozzarella, sliced
2 oz. cherry tomatoes
Season chopped basil and thyme
Salt and pepper to season

Place thin slices of heirloom on plate. Place sliced mozzarella on top of tomatoes and then place prosciutto on top of mozzarella. Toss cherry and tear drop tomatoes in salt and pepper olive oil and place on top of salad.

Vinaigrette:
2 oz. balsamic vinegar
2 oz. honey

4 oz. olive oil
1 oz. whole grain mustard

Combine all ingredients and emulsify.

Submitted by: Johnson Tan, Owner & Executive Chef

Pappy's Place

943 N. Main Avenue
Springfield, MO 65802
417-866-8744

Pappy's Place has stood at this location since 1904. While now housing a bar/restaurant, the store first began as a family-owned shoe repair shop. Shortly after that, the owners opened a grocery store and kept it that way until the 1920s.

New owners opened a cafe on the property in 1924. Following Prohibition, the cafe applied for a beer-by-the-drink license. This license, which is still held by Pappy's, is the oldest continuous license in Springfield.

Pappy's Place may be old, and not very well-known, but it is a place of character. The people are friendly, the food is good and the beer is cold. A casual atmosphere makes for a laid-back time. For many people, it is a place of good memories.

Chef Jack's Cous Cous Salad

I was never fond of Italian foods until I started cooking it. Cous cous is not Italian,
but these flavors work well with this healthy salad. MAN! Is it good!

1 pkg. plain cous cous
1 zucchini, diced, seeds removed
1 yellow squash, diced, seeds removed
1/2 c. fresh parsley, chopped
1/3 c. virgin olive oil
Salt and pepper
Parmesan cheese, grated

1/2 red onion, diced
1 tomato
1 red bell pepper, diced
3 cloves fresh garlic, chopped
2 lemons, juiced and zested
1/3 c. fresh basil, chiffonade cut

Prepare cous cous according to directions. Set aside. In a mixing bowl, add vegetables. Do not remove skins of zucchini and squash. (They add nutrition and great color.) Throw in the parsley, then stir in the garlic, olive oil and lemon juice and zest, along with the basil. Smell it; season it with salt and pepper; now taste it. It should really be flavorful and Italian in aroma. If it's too bland, season with more salt. Mix in cous cous. Top every portion (or entrée portion) with shredded parmesan cheese.

Submitted by: Jack Rauhoff, Chef

Riad Mediterranean Cuisine

105 Park Central Square
Springfield, MO 65806
417-866-1151

1250 E. Republic
Springfield, MO 65806
417-881-RIAD (7423)

www.riadcuisine.com

Since opening in February of 2004, Riad cuisine has proudly given the Springfield area a taste of the Mediterranean. With the health conscious menu, customers can enjoy a tasty meal without guilt. Meeting rooms are available at both locations. Our private rooms are conveniently located and tastefully decorated with various seating arrangements that can accommodate your needs. Ideal for meetings, parties, receptions, conferences, or retreats. Optional services include complete meals, catering, high speed internet, projection screen, TV with cable and bar service. Call to reserve.

Tabbouleh

1 c. Bulgur wheat
1/2 c. tomatoes, diced
1 c. parsley, chopped
1 tsp. salt

2. c. water
1/2 c. cucumber, diced
1/4 c. lemon juice
3 cloves garlic, minced

Pour 1 cup of dry bulgur wheat into a medium size container with lid. Pour 2 cup of water into the same container and close the lid. Set aside and wait four hours, allowing the wheat to absorb water. The wheat will double in size. Once wheat is soft, pour into a medium size mixing bowl. Add the rest of ingredients. Mix together and set aside for 5 minutes. Mix together again and taste. If needed, add more lemon juice or salt.

Submitted by: Rachel Hopper, Manager

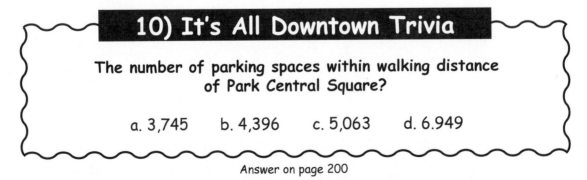

10) It's All Downtown Trivia

The number of parking spaces within walking distance of Park Central Square?

a. 3,745   b. 4,396   c. 5,063   d. 6.949

Answer on page 200

St. Michaels

An Educational Sports Bar & Grill
301 South Avenue
Springfield, MO 65806
417-865-2315

Although the names have changed over the past 36 years, the style remains consistent. Owner/operators Nick and Jenny Russo have a long standing history in the local restaurant industry. St. Michael's, located at the corner of South and McDaniel, in Springfield, MO, has evolved from Pop's Malt shop, Ebbets field (both the Cherry Street and Walnut Street locations) and Russo's Café and Market. Their most recent project is an intimate (65-70 seat) sports eatery located in the heart of the downtown revival. Jenny, a former Kansas City resident, operates St. Michael's during the daytime hours and has developed a reputation for her fresh soups and gourmet sandwiches and currently boasts that she can make 3 sandwiches to her husband's one. Three to two may be a more realistic ratio. St. Michael's continues with their tradition of serving fresh 1/2 lb. burgers and fresh-cut fries. The restaurant is available for private gatherings while catering is also available.

Fresh Mozzarella and Tomato Salad with Fresh Basil

One large fresh mozzarella ball
3-4 leaves of fresh basil
Imported balsamic vinegar
Salt and pepper

2 home grown tomatoes (if available)
Extra virgin olive oil
Picarino Romano cheese

Slice the mozzarella ball and place on a plate; top with fresh tomato slices and leaves of fresh basil. Salt and pepper to taste. Place olive oil and balsamic vinegar in a blender (5 portions of oil to 1 portion of vinegar), blend until consistent, no separation. Drizzle over the salad and top with Romano cheese. Serve with Italian bread.

Submitted by: Nick & Jenny Russo, Owners

The Grotto

3046 S. Kimbrough
Springfield, MO
417-886-9600

www.gogrotto.com

Fresh Ingredients and Fresh ideas. That is what we think makes our food so unique and great tasting. We here at The Grotto strive to use the highest quality ingredients and create one of a kind combinations that both taste and look great. Great for families, business lunches, or casual dinners, The Grotto always has something for everyone!!!

The Grotto Salad Mix

1 head of romaine
1 head of leaf lettuce

5 oz. pkg. Spring Mix or Mesculun Greens

In your kitchen sink, (after you have thoroughly washed and sanitized it), plug the sink and add enough ice to fill about 1/4 of the sink. Crushed ice works best since it will dissolve easier and more quickly. Fill the sink about 2/3 full. The water temperature should be around 34-36° F. If you can barely stand having your hand submersed for less than 30 seconds, it is cold enough. If the ice has not dissolved, then use a strainer to remove.

Inspect your lettuce. Remove any leaves that are brown or damaged. Using a very sharp knife, cut down the length of the romaine head in sections between the ribs of the leaves. Proceed to cut across the head of romaine, creating squares that are about an inch in size. As you are cutting the squares, push the lettuce in the ice bath. Repeat the above steps with the head of leaf. Then add the package of Spring Mix/Mesculun Greens. Agitate the mixture in the ice bath to remove dirt, chemicals and potential bacteria. This is referred to as "shocking" the lettuce.

If you have a lettuce spinner, simply spin until dry. Otherwise use a strainer and shake until as dry as possible. All you need are your favorite dressings and toppings and you will have a great salad every time!!!

Submitted by: Mark Coleman, Owner

Breads/Breakfast & Sandwiches

Anton's Coffee Shop

Anton's Coffee Shop

937 S. Glenstone Ave.
Springfield, MO 65802
417-869-7681

Anton's is one of Springfield's oldest operating restaurants, owned by Anton and Roberta Tasich since 1974. Known for -"Breakfast Served All Day." There is a full menu of breakfast and lunch items. "People can get a hamburger for breakfast or oatmeal for lunch." Breakfast orders make up more than 80 percent of their business, where the omelets rule! Anton's menu features over 30 varieties of omelets plus a daily special. Most everything is still made fresh from scratch; the staff even grinds the coffee beans fresh. Hours: 6 am - 2 pm six days a week; 8 am - 2 pm Sunday; Closed Tuesday.

Southwestern Quiche

Crust:
1/2 (11 oz.) pkg. pie crust mix
1 Tbsp. cold water

1 tsp. chili powder

Filling:
2/3 c. cheddar cheese, grated
3 large eggs, slightly beaten
1/4 tsp. white pepper
1- 4 oz. can green chilies, diced
2 Tbsp. green onions, finely chopped

1/2 c. Monterrey Jack cheese, grated
1 tsp. salt
1-1/2 c. half and half
2-1/4 oz. can ripe olives, sliced

Pre-heat oven to 350º. In a medium bowl, blend pie crust mix, chili powder and water. Mix with fork until dough holds together. Form into a smooth ball; roll dough on floured surface until it is 1-1/2 inches larger than inverted 9 inch pie pan. Ease into pan and flute the edges. Mix cheese together, spread on bottom of pastry shell. In medium size bowl, mix eggs, salt, pepper, cream, chiles, olives and green onions. Pour over cheese covered pastry. Bake 40-45 minutes until inserted knife comes out clean. Serve at once.

Submitted by: Anton Tasich, Owner

**Big Momma's Coffee
& Espresso Bar**

217 E Commercial St
Springfield, MO 65803
417-865-9911

www.bigmommascoffee.com

You have to get up very early to get the first cup of coffee at Big Momma's Coffee House and Espresso Bar in Springfield. Located on the often overlooked Commercial Street Historic district, owner Lyle Foster; a Chicago native, was initially interested in refurbishing a building into loft apartments. Then he had an epiphany. "I believe in the notion of a 3rd place. Everybody has a job, a home, and they need a third place to hang out. And that should be a coffee shop." With that in mind, Big Momma's was born.

You never know who you'll run into at Big Momma's. From students and business people to city leaders and artists -- people stream in day and night. The walls feature works from local photographers and artists. Momma's Back Porch hosts dinner theater regularly and live jazz on Tuesdays.

Momma Joe's Life Changing Blueberry Muffins

4 c. all purpose flour
1/2 tsp. salt
2 eggs
1-1/2 c. whole milk

1-1/2 c. sugar
4 level tsp. baking powder
2/3 c. vegetable oil
1 to 1-1/2 c. berries

Topping:
2 Tbsp. flour
1/2 tsp. cinnamon

4 Tbsp. sugar
4 Tbsp. cold butter

In large mixing bowl stir all dry ingredients. Beat eggs, oil and milk together. Add to dry ingredients. Stir just until blended. Fold in the blueberries. Mixing too much makes the muffins tough. Let batter sit while the topping is prepared. In small bowl mix all dry ingredients. Cut in cold butter until mixture is coarse. Pour or spoon batter into extra large muffin tin. Sprinkle on topping. Bake in 375° oven for about 30 minutes, or until tops are slightly resistant to the touch.

Submitted by: Joe Terry, Barista and Baker

Cassils Cafes Inc.

2925 W. Republic Rd.
Springfield, MO 65807
417-851-1104

2601 N. Cresthaven
Springfield, MO 65803
417-866-2221

www.cassils.com

Cassils is your neighborhood gathering place. Whether it's stopping by on the way to work for a latte and fresh cinnamon roll, taking a client to lunch, studying for finals on your laptop, having dinner with your family, or enjoying live entertainment with your friends, Cassils is your place.

At Cassils, we started by bringing to Springfield some of the best coffees the world has to offer, roasted and blended by some of the best roasters in the country. We added to that our award-winning menu of unique, casual appetizers, entrees, baked goodies, and desserts. We serve it all up in a comfortable, friendly atmosphere you're going to love.

Roast Beef Panini

4 slices roast beef (about 3 oz.)
1/4 c. onions and sweet peppers, sliced
Olive oil

2 slices Swiss cheese
2 slices ciabatta
Dried basil

Slice the onions and peppers (use a mixture of sweet red, yellow, orange, and green) into thin strips. Sauté the onions and peppers with olive oil until the onions are translucent and the peppers are tender. Just before these are done, place the roast beef on top until warmed. Place the roast beef on a slice of ciabatta, then top with the onion and peppers. Place the cheese on top and cover with the other slice of ciabatta. Brush the bread lightly with olive oil and sprinkle lightly with dried basil. Grill until golden and the cheese begins to melt.

Wolf's Point Ham & Swiss

4 slices lean ham (about 3 oz.)
2 slices sourdough bread
1 leaf lettuce

2 slices Swiss cheese
2 slices tomato
1 Tbsp. raspberry preserves

Spread the raspberry preserves on one slice of sourdough. Stack the ham, lettuce, tomato, and cheese on that slice of bread. Top with the other slice of bread and grill until golden and the cheese just begins to melt. It's just like the ham and cheese I had growing up on the farm, near Wolf's Point, Missouri.

Submitted by: Kevin Cassil, Country-boy, Scientist, and Restaurant Owner

Clary's Restaurant

900 E Battlefield Rd
Springfield, MO 65804
417-866-6200

www.eatatclarys.com

The relationship between Farmer, Fisherman and Chef coupled with the evolution of rapid airfreight, has revolutionized the restaurant industry, particularly among fine dining restaurants. At Clary's we now buy produce, poultry, and meat directly from local farmers. We order fish directly from the West coast, Hawaii, and the Gulf of Mexico, and it is flown overnight from the location to your table. We get produce flown to us overnight the day it is picked in California. Our menu now changes regularly to reflect the products we are getting in daily! Our philosophy has not changed, that is, to provide you with the most exciting dining experience possible.

Crepes with Mixed Berries in Grand Marnier

For the crepes:

3/4 c. flour
1 Tbsp. sugar
3 Tbsp. butter
2 eggs

1/2 tsp. salt
1/2 tsp. vanilla extract
1 c. milk

Place flour and salt in food processor and pulse to mix. Melt butter in milk in small saucepan over low heat. Add milk mixture to flour, running processor constantly to blend well. Add eggs one at a time and blend well. Let batter sit for at least 30 minutes before using. To cook crepes, heat a 6 inch non-stick pan until sizzling. Spray pan with pan release. Pour 1 ounce of batter in pan and swirl until batter coats bottom of pan (very thin!). Cook for about one minute or until you can see the edges of the crepe turning brown. Remove crepe and place on parchment paper to cool.

For the berries:

2 Tbsp. butter
1/2 c. sugar

1 pt. mixed berries (drain well if using frozen)
1/4 c. Grand Marnier or other orange liqueur

Heat a small saucepan over medium high heat and add butter. Cook blueberries in butter until they begin to burst. Add sugar and continue to cook until sauce thickens. Add liqueur and cook until desired consistency is reached. Pour warm over crepes and garnish with whipped cream and fresh mint.

Submitted by: James Clary, Owner & Executive Chef

Cooks Kettle Restaurant

At Victory Trade School
200 W. Commercial
Springfield, MO 65803
417-864-2210

www.victorytradeschool.org

The Bed and breakfast French toast is a set I designed for KY3 morning show for 2007 Mothers day breakfast in bed. I cooked the entire dish on live TV staging different parts to make the timing come out to fill the 5.5 minutes they gave me that morning. It is tricky to have the food come out within several segments on a live TV show. I think even worse than having to hurry to make it was the time I got done early and had to make unexpected small talk with the camera in my face. I am sure I sounded like a genius that day.

Bed and Breakfast Style French Toast with Glazed Strawberries & Ginger Cream

4 slices of thick cut bread (wheat, white, French or sour dough)
1 tsp. vanilla
2 Tbsp. oil
4 eggs, beaten
1/2 tsp. cinnamon, ground

Mix together the eggs, cinnamon, and vanilla. Batter each side of the bread in the egg mixture. Cook it on medium heat with the oil in a non-stick pan until it is golden brown.

Glazed Strawberries:
5 c. fresh strawberries, quarters
1 Tbsp. cornstarch
1/2 c. sugar
1 Tbsp. water

Take two cups of the strawberries and purée them in a food processor or blender. Place the pureed strawberries in saucepot with the sugar. Simmer for 3-5 minutes. Mix together the cornstarch and water then add it to the cooking strawberries and bring back to a simmer. Strain this glaze through a fine strainer to remove the seeds. Let the glaze cool 15 minutes then fold in the rest of the strawberries. Refrigerate for several hours before they are served.

Ginger Cream:
1 c. heavy cream
1 tsp. ground ginge
2 Tbsp. powder sugar
1/2 tsp. vanilla

Combine the cream, vanilla, and ginger in a mixing bowl. Use a wire whip to beat the whip cream to soft peaks. Sift in the powder sugar and whip until peaks stiffen.

Submitted by: Chadwick Isom, Executive Chef

Downtown Springfield Association

304 W McDaniel St
Springfield, MO 65806
417-831-6200

www.itsalldowntown.com

Easy Cheese Danish

2 pkg. refrigerated crescent roll dough
1 c. sugar
2 tsp. vanilla

2-8 oz. pkg. cream cheese, softened
1 egg

Topping:
1/2 c. butter or margarine
1/2 c. chopped pecans

1/2 c. sugar
1 tsp. cinnamon

Preheat oven to 350°. Grease a 9 x 13 inch baking dish. Unroll one can of crescent roll dough and press into the bottom of the baking dish, pressing the seams together forming a flat sheet and easing the edges halfway up the side of the pan.

Combine cream cheese, sugar, egg and vanilla blending until smooth. Spread cream cheese mixture over dough. Using wax paper or plastic wrap, tear off a sheet as long as the baking pan. Unroll dough onto sheet and press seems together. Place another sheet of wax paper or plastic wrap on top. With a rolling pin roll out dough so that it is large enough to cover cream cheese mixture. Remove one of the wax paper/plastic wrap sheets and lay on top of cream cheese mixture. Remove second sheet and tuck the edges in to seal in cream cheese mixture.

In a small sauce pan melt butter/margarine over low heat. Add sugar and stir until dissolved then add cinnamon and pecans. Pour topping mixture over the top of the dough and spread to cover. (Work gently so as not to tear the dough).

Bake about 30 minutes or until golden. Butter/margarine tends to pool so check frequently to evenly distribute. Let stand to cool. Cut into squares and serve.

Note:
This dish really needs to cool thoroughly or cream cheese mixture will be too runny. This Danish is great refrigerated or reheated in the microwave to desired temperature.

Add-ins: You can add a 1/2 cup of your favorite jam/preserves and swirl through cream cheese mixture or add 1/2 to 3/4 cup of fresh blueberries, raspberries or strawberries.

Submitted by: Kathryn Vicat-Dlabach, UDA Community Development & Festival Assistant

Ebbets Field
Restaurant & Pub

1027 E. Walnut Street
Springfield, MO 65806
417-865-5050

You never know who you'll run into at Ebbets Field. University students, sports fans, construction workers and those negotiating big business take in food and drink at our restaurant and pub. With a long and colorful history, Ebbets field is many things to many amazing people: a family favorite, a haven for all things sports and part of amazing memories of your "best" years.

We take great pride in our menu offering from our steaks and burgers, pizza, soups and salads all made fresh daily. Aside from your food, our philosophy at Ebbets is to try and not take things too seriously. Remember: we live in the greatest country in the world, and for you locals, take pride because we're from the great state of Missouri.

Cajun Po' Boy Wrap

2 - 4 oz. deep fried cod fillets
1/2 c. mayonnaise
1 (10 to 12 inch) tortilla wrap (soft)

1/4 c. shredded cheddar cheese
1 Tbsp. Redhot sauce

Take two pieces of deep-fried cod fillets and place them on a soft tortilla wrap with the melted cheddar on it. The cheddar cheese will easily melt on the wrap when put in the microwave for 30-40 seconds. Mix the mayonnaise with the Redhot sauce to create your Cajun sauce. Next, pour the Cajun sauce on top of the pieces of fish. Finally, wrap up the tortilla and serve.

Stephanie Haley's World Famous Fresh Chicken Salad Sandwiches

1 red onion, chopped
1-1/2 c. ranch dressing
Pinch of salt
8 chicken breasts, diced
Your favorite bread
Leaf lettuce

1 c. celery, chopped
1 Tbsp. parsley
Pinch of ground pepper
Lemon pepper seasoning
2 sliced tomatoes

Lightly dust chicken breasts with lemon pepper seasoning and charbroil. Chill the chicken once it's grilled. Mix chopped red onion, chopped celery, ranch dressing, parsley, salt and pepper. Add chilled chicken chunks and mix well. Toast bread of choice. If desired, add chicken salad, tomato slices and leaf lettuce. Makes approximately 12-14 sandwiches.

Submitted by: Lance D. "Itchy" Reeves, Proprietor

First Friday Art Walk

411 N. Sherman Parkway
Springfield, Missouri 65802
417-849-8255

www.ffaw.org

First Friday Art Walk, held 6-10 p.m. the first Friday of each month, is a free walking tour of downtown Springfield's 20-plus art galleries. The event features works by local, regional and national artists, as well as live demonstrations and performances, all in support of First Friday Art Walk's nonprofit mission of promoting fine art and economic vitality in the Downtown Arts District. For more information, give us a call or visit our website.

Brie-and-Sausage Breakfast Casserole

1 - 8 oz. round Brie*
6 white sandwich bread slices
7 lg. eggs, divided
2 c. fat-free milk
1 tsp. seasoned salt

1 lb. ground hot pork sausage
1 c. parmesan cheese, grated
3 c. whipping cream, divided
1 Tbsp. fresh sage, chopped or 1 tsp. dried rubbed sage
1 tsp. dry mustard

* 2 cups shredded Swiss cheese may be substituted if you don't have Brie

Garnishes:
Green onions, chopped

Parmesan cheese, shaved

Trim rind from Brie and discard; cut cheese into cubes and set aside. Cook sausage in a large skillet over medium-high heat, stirring until it crumbles and is no longer pink; drain well.
Cut crusts from bread slices and place crusts evenly in bottom of a lightly greased 13 x 9 inch baking dish. Layer evenly with bread slices, sausage, Brie and parmesan cheese.
Whisk together 5 eggs, 2 cups whipping cream and next 4 ingredients; pour evenly over cheeses. Cover and chill mixture for 8 hours. Whisk together remaining 2 eggs and remaining 1 cup whipping cream; pour evenly over chilled mixture. Bake at 350° for 1 hour or until casserole is set. Garnish, if desired. Serves 8 to 10.

Submitted by: Sandra CH Smith, Innkeeper & Exec. Director, Springfield Regional Arts Council

Galloway Station
Bar & Grill

4211 S. Lone Pine Ave
Springfield Mo 65804
417-881-9730

myspace.com/gallowaystation

Hidden in the middle of southwest Springfield and part of historic Galloway Village, Galloway Station has Springfield's best outdoor dining patio. The view is relaxed and calming. The Galloway Trail and its walkers, joggers, and bikers etc. are always passing by traveling from Sequiota Park. You can also see the railroad tracks as the building itself is an old historic train station. The decor and charm of the building still keeps true to its heritage. With a tasty menu, cold beer, and live music on the weekends, you really can't go wrong with Galloway Station.

Rajin Cajun Burger

1/2 lb Angus beef
2 slices Swiss cheese
2 slices crisp bacon
1 slice red onion, optional

1 Lg. sesame seed bun, sliced
Cajun and steak seasoning
2 slices tomato
Leaf lettuce

Pattie and season the meat. Grill burger to desired temperature. Just before removing meat from grill, add bacon and top with cheese until cheese has melted bacon to burger. Build your burger up with tomato, onion and leaf lettuce.

Submitted by: John Tsahiridis, Manager

11) It's All Downtown Trivia

Where was Route 66 officially named in Springfield?

a. Colonial House

b. Woodruff Building

c. Shrine Mosque

d. Gillioz Theatre

Answer on page 200

Taste of Springfield

A Collection of Restaurant Recipes from the Queen City of the Ozarks

This wonderful project would not have been possible without the featured independent and locally owned restaurants in this cookbook, plus the support from these local businesses...

THANK YOU!

Harter House ~

Famous For Our Meats
The Finest Quality Dry Aged Meat,
Aged Cheese & Specialty Items

Welcome to Harter House Supermarket, a company dedicated to offering the
finest ingredients for your dining pleasure. Our philosophy is simple... we only
sell the highest quality productsYou'll see and taste the difference when
you experience our old-fashioned neighborhood market.
Quality meats and great service.

Quality Meats

Harter House Supermarkets

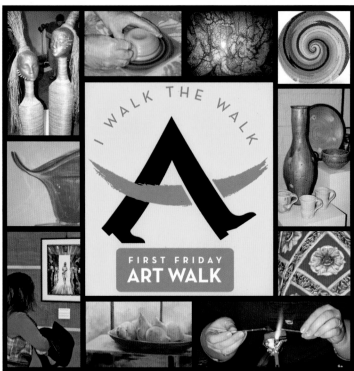

Experts in
##
health

At CoxHealth, you'll find a team of professionals specializing in all aspects of women's wellness. That includes fitness and nutrition experts, specialists in high-risk mother/baby care and an outstanding cardiovascular health team. We lead the way in cancer treatment, stroke care and diabetes management. Here you'll find the region's best resources for behavioral health, osteoporosis care, midlife health and the special concerns of senior women.

For more than 20 years, The Women's Center at CoxHealth has been a leading voice for women's health. We were the first women's center in the region, and you can still turn to us for your health answers.

Need help finding a physician who's right for you? **Give us a call at 269-INFO or 269-LADY.**

→ Special Delivery maternity program

→ Parenting e-mail newsletter

→ Breast Care Clinic

→ Osteoporosis Clinic

→ Joyce Schwandt Resource Library

→ Milestones Boutique

→ Physician Referrals

→ Women's health educators

→ Health programs and classes throughout the year

coxhealth.com

Experts. Friends. Neighbors.

Sonya and Tom are *COOKING!*

Weekdays 5-7am

Start your day with
Sonya Kullman and Tom Trtan
News and Weather

COVERAGE YOU CAN COUNT ON

EVERY WEEKDAY!

SERVICE THE WAY YOU WANT IT

A Division of **Reinhart** FoodService

Banta Foods is a full line distributor offering a complete line of products that can be tailored for any operation.

We also customize our services and solutions to go along with each and every category of products.

Our total commitment to creating and maintaining a successful partnership with you means we deliver more to your table than anyone else.

More high quality products, more value-added services and more innovative solutions.

Proud Sponsor of the Taste of Springfield!

1960

1962 Jezzard Fruit Co. changes to **JEZZARD-BANTA FRUIT CO.** Mr. Banta, after a full year of negotiation, purchases Jezzard Fruit Company and changes the name to JEZZARD-BANTA FRUIT CO.

1963 Jezzard-Banta Fruit Co. changes to **BANTA FRUIT CO.**

1980

1984 Banta Fruit Co. changes to **BANTA FOODS, INC.** Mr. Banta changes the name to better reflect the company's move to full-line distribution.

2000

AFTER MORE THAN A CENTURY OF SERVICE, THE GOAL OF BANTA FOODS REMAINS UNCHANGED, TO CONTINUE **DELIVERING MORE TO THE TABLE.**

...53 ...d and Sons ...es to ...RUIT CO. ...mes a closed ...nd changes ...me.

...nta advances ...position of ...l manager.

During the late **1960's** BANTA changes its emphasis from retail to the food-service industry.

1980's and beyond... BANTA FOODS is a full-line foodservice distributor, marketing a complete array of food products, supplies, chemicals, paper goods, equipment and smallwares.

1982 BANTA computerizes its operation.

1984 BANTA moves to 1620 N. Packer Road.

1988 BANTA joins FROSTY ACRES Buying Cooperative.

1993 Customer Presentation Facility completed.

1994 BANTA joins UNIPRO, the largest broadline and systems cooperative distribution group in the world. With more than 200 members in nearly every state of the nation, and in the Caribbean, Japan and Australia, UniPro membership purchases from more than 800 suppliers worldwide.

1995 BANTA's 100th Year

BANTA FOODS

DELIVERING MORE TO THE TABLE™

The Largest Family Owned Full Line Food Distributor in Missouri, Arkansas, Kansas, and Oklahoma

"Your Independent Option"

Assisting Food Service Operators in Achieving their Financial Goals for over 100 years

1.800.492.2682

A Division of

WWW.BANTAFOODS.COM • 1620 N. Packer Rd. Springfield, Mo. 65803

sushi • fresh seafood • natural & organic foods • Midwestern Gold beef
Creekstone Farms beef • Farmland All Natural pork • wine, beer and spirits

Price Cutter
www.PriceCutterOnline.com

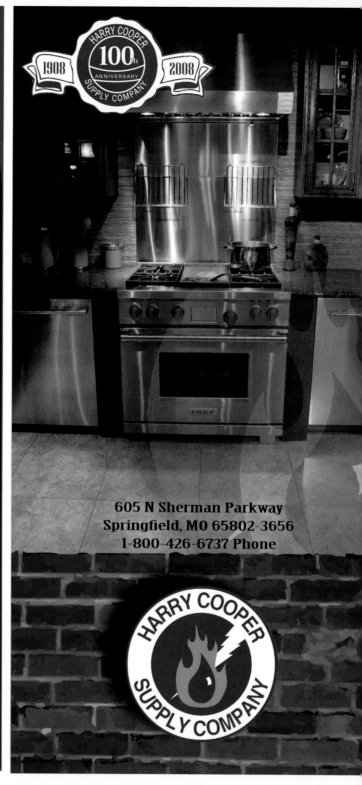

FASHIONABLY FLAVORFUL

itsalldowntown.com

Proud to Host the Taste of Springfield

Honey Heaven & the Vineyard Tea Room

2516 S Campbell
Springfield, MO 65807
417-869-0233

www.honeyheaven.com

White Chocolate and Amaretto Honey Twists

1/3 c. Honey Heaven's Golden, Glorious & Pure Honey
2 Tbsp. fresh lemon juice
1-1/2 tsp. salt
1 c. (2 sticks) unsalted butter, room temperature
3 lg. eggs
2 tsp. finely grated lemon peel
1-2 squares of white almond bark

4 Tbsp. anise-flavored liqueur
4-1/4 c. all purpose flour
1 tsp. baking powder
1 c. sugar
1-1/2 Tbsp. anise seed
1/8 c. crumbled sliced almonds

Glaze:
Mix honey, two tablespoons liqueur and lemon juice in small bowl. Set glaze aside.

Preheat oven to 350°. Lightly butter baking sheets. Combine flour, salt, and baking powder in medium bowl. Using electric mixer, beat butter and sugar in large bowl until fluffy. Add eggs, one at a time, beating well after each addition. Beat in remaining two tablespoons liqueur, almonds and lemon peel. Gradually mix in dry ingredients. Working with one tablespoon of dough at a time, roll dough between palms and work surface into 7 inch ropes. Form into bow ties or twists. Place on prepared baking sheets, spacing evenly. Brush glaze over cookies. Bake cookies until pale golden, about 15 minutes. Transfer cookies to racks. Lightly brush cookies again with glaze and drizzle with melted white almond bark, then top with crumbled almonds.. Cool. Store in airtight container at room temperature up to one week or freeze up to one month.

Submitted by: Lena Meyer, "The Honey Lady"

The Mudhouse

323 South Ave
Springfield, MO 65806
417-832-1720

www.mudhousecoffee.com

When it comes to the way Mudhouse Coffee does business, one word says it all. "Freshness." With coffee, and enjoying a delicious cup of coffee, freshness is the only thing that really matters. What we can guarantee to our customers is that Mudhouse Coffee will be the freshest coffee available. We micro roast our coffee in small batches when we need it, so you never have to worry about our coffee sitting and losing the crucial freshness that is so important. It doesn't matter whether you purchase our coffee inside the coffeehouse or from the website; we guarantee it will be the freshest, best tasting coffee available! Open Monday-Friday 7:00am - Midnight, Saturday 7:00am - Midnight and Sunday 8:30am - 11:00pm.

Mudhouse Berry Scones

This is my twist on the traditional English Scone. They go fantastic with a cup of Mudhouse Coffee or English Breakfast Tea (or Guinness).

2 c. butter
10 c. flour
1 c. fresh blueberries
1 c. fresh strawberries

2-1/2 c. sugar
1/2 c. baking powder
1 c. fresh raspberries
Half and half

Microwave butter for 2 minutes. Mix butter and sugar until well blended. Mix the flour and the baking powder with whisk. Blend the flour/baking powder to the butter/sugar mix. Add half and half until the mix has reached the desired consistency. Measure out 6 ounces of batter to make 4-6 scones. Smash the batter flat with the palm of your hand. Place berries of choice on top of scone. Top with cinnamon and raw sugar. Bake at 325°. Scones will be done in around 20-25 minutes. Make sure the centers aren't raw and rotate at least once to get them to bake evenly.

Submitted by: Brian King, Co-owner

Pappy's Place

943 N. Main Avenue
Springfield, MO 65802
417-866-8744

Pappy's Place has stood at this location since 1904. While now housing a bar/restaurant, the store first began as a family-owned shoe repair shop. Shortly after that, the owners opened a grocery store and kept it that way until the 1920s.

New owners opened a cafe on the property in 1924. Following Prohibition, the cafe applied for a beer-by-the-drink license. This license, which is still held by Pappy's, is the oldest continuous license in Springfield.

Pappy's Place may be old, and not very well-known, but it is a place of character. The people are friendly, the food is good and the beer is cold. A casual atmosphere makes for a laid-back time. For many people, it is a place of good memories.

Chicken Liver Omelet

Bob McCroskey is a good friend of mine. He owns his own real estate business in the Springfield area. He feels pretty comfortable "pesterin" me for special dishes. He ate chicken liver omelet when he was younger, and asked for it. I had no idea what to do as I've never imagined such a thing, but I tried this.

4 oz. chicken livers, sautéed in butter
1 clove garlic, chopped
Salt and pepper
1 Tbsp. cream
Parsley, chopped

2 Tbsp. onion, chopped
Hot pepper flakes
3 eggs
Sprinkle of feta cheese
Tomato, chopped

Soak the livers in milk over night. Sauté the livers for about 4 minutes, then add onions and garlic when livers are cooked. Coarsely chop everything and reserve. Beat eggs with cream. Pour into an omelet pan that has been sprayed with a "nonstick" spray. As the eggs start to cook into a solid form, add liver mixture, pepper flakes, and salt and pepper. Fold eggs into omelet shape with a spatula. Top each omelet with feta cheese, chopped parsley and chopped tomato.

Submitted by: Jack Rauhoff, Chef

Recipe Publishers

2049 E. Cherry Street
Springfield, MO 65802
417-873-2267

www.recipepubs.com

Recipe Publishers is based in the beautiful Ozarks city of Springfield, Missouri. We produce, publish and help promote many kinds of cookbooks: *Family's Favorites, Fundraiser Cookbooks, Chefs' Collections, Restaurant Recipes, Sports Teams Cookbooks. plus many more.* **"If You Can Cook It - We Can Print It."** We'll help with each step in the process of creating the best cookbooks possible.

Moms Christmas Morning Cinnamon Rolls

Growing up, my mom would get up very early (when she heard Santa) so she could get the rolls into the oven so when my brother and sisters would wake, we would have hot homemade cinnamon rolls for Christmas morning.

Dough:

2 c. water
1 c. sugar
2 large eggs
1 pkg. yeast

1/2 c. shortening (Crisco)
2 tsp. salt
3 c. flour (more as needed)

In a sauce pan, bring water to a boil. Add shortening, sugar and salt. Let this come to room temperature. Add yeast and stir. Add 1 egg at a time, mix between each egg. Slowly add 1 cup of flour, make sure it is completely mixed in with no lumps. Continue adding 1 more cup of flour, slowly. Start mixing with dough hook on low. Add remaining flour. Make sure you don't add to much flour, use your hands to make sure it is not to dry (it should be sticky to the touch). Grease a large bowl then add dough and cover with a dish towel, set on a warm stove. Punch down 2 to 3 times throughout the evening.

Rolls:

1 pd. butter, softened
2 Tbsp. ground cinnamon

3 c. brown sugar

About 9:30-10pm, roll out dough on floured surface into 2 - 12 x 18 inch rectangles. Spread soft butter over entire dough surface. Add 1-1/2 cups of brown sugar and sprinkle 1 tablespoon cinnamon to each surface. Roll length wise as tight as you can. Cut from the center. Cuts need to be at least 1-1/2 inches apart. Spray 2 - 9 x 13 inch pans with non-stick spray. Push tail from the center of each roll under the rolls so it does not pop out while cooking. Bake at 350°, start watching after 18 minutes. Yields: 24

Icing:

2-1/2 c. powdered sugar
Mix until icing is thin to your liking.

1/4 c. hot strong coffee

Submitted by: Judie Cornwell, Cookbook Advisor & Publishers Mom

The Grotto

3046 S. Kimbrough
Springfield, MO
417-886-9600

www.gogrotto.com

"Fresh Ingredients and Fresh ideas." That is what we think makes our food so unique and great tasting. We here at The Grotto strive to use the highest quality ingredients and create one of a kind combinations that both taste and look great. Great for families, business lunches, or casual dinners, The Grotto always has something for everyone!!!

The Grotto Pizza Dough

1 pkg. active dry or fresh yeast
1 c. warm water (105-115° F)
1 tsp. kosher salt

1 tsp. honey
3 c. all purpose flour
1 Tbsp. extra-virgin olive oil, plus additional for brushing

In a small bowl, dissolve the yeast and honey in 1/4 cup warm water. In a larger bowl, combine the flour and the salt. Add the oil, the yeast mixture, and the remaining 3/4 cup of water and mix until the dough forms a ball. (The pizza dough can also be made in a mixer fitted with a dough hook. Mix on low speed until the mixture comes cleanly away from the sides of the bowl and starts to climb up the dough hook.)

Alternate method:
If you have a bread machine, use the dough setting and let it mix. Remove after the mixing is done. Turn the dough out onto a clean work surface and knead by hand 2-3 minutes longer. The dough should be smooth and firm. Cover the dough and let it rise in a cool spot for about 2 hours. (When ready, the dough will stretch as it is lightly pulled.) Divide the dough into 6 balls, about 4 ounces each. Work each ball by pulling down the sides and tucking under the bottom of the ball. Repeat 4 or 5 times. Then on a smooth, un-floured surface, roll the ball under the palm of your hand until the top of the dough is smooth and firm, about 1 minute.

Submitted by: Mark Coleman, Owner

Tower Club

The Hammons Tower
901 E Saint Louis St # 2100
Springfield, MO 65806
(417) 866-4466

www.towerclubspringfield.com

Main Dining room hours: Tuesday through Friday, 11 a.m. - 2 p.m. Top of the Tower Dining Room: Tuesday through Thursday, 5 p.m. - 9 p.m. Friday and Saturday, 5 p.m. - 10 p.m. Closed on Sundays and Mondays

The Club will accommodate private parties during regular hours of operation. Special arrangements may be made for parties outside of normal Club hours with Club Manager.

Amenities: Finest food and service. Exquisite dining room and lounge. Panoramic view of the city. Special promotions. Five private suites seat up to 30. Starlight Room accommodates up to 150 people. Reciprocity at over 150 clubs throughout the world.

A Gentle Reminder: Please make reservations for lunch and dinner before coming to The Club. It helps us serve you better.

Smoked Turkey Crepes

Crepe Shell:
1 medium crepe shell
1 tsp. olive oil

1 medium egg, whipped

Crepe Filling:
2 medium mushrooms, washed and sliced
3 medium asparagus spears
1/2 c. fresh spinach, cleaned
1/2 c. smoked turkey breast

1/4 c. red onion, julienne
1 tsp. garlic, minced
1-1/2 tsp. olive oil
1/4 c. grated provolone cheese

Heat olive oil in omelet pan. Add medium egg. Add crepe shell and let brown. Then flip and cook until egg is done. Set crepe shell aside. Then in another sauté pan, heat oil on medium heat and add mushrooms and red onions. Cook for 1 minute. Then add garlic, asparagus, and spinach. When spinach has wilted, add smoked turkey, pinch of salt and pepper. Add filling to half of the crepe shell. Top with cheese and fold over. Microwave for 20-30 seconds until cheese has melted. Serve with hash browns or potato cakes.

Submitted by: Brad Lyons, C.E.C., Executive Chef

Waves of Grain Artisan Breads

Springfield, Missouri
417-894-1190

wavesofgrain@mchsi.com

Having recently retired from the day-to-day operations of his boutique bakery, Chef Dreshfield now spends his time as a college instructor in the local community teaching at Drury University, Missouri State University, and Ozarks Technical Community College. From "Fundamentals of Baking to Integrated Marketing Communications Strategies," Chef Dreshfield provides his students with a unique perspective on the Hospitality Industry. He is a food service manufacturer's consultant as well.

Classic French Bread

2 lbs. 10 oz. bread flour
1 Tbsp. instant yeast

24 oz. warm water
1 Tbsp. salt

These four ingredients are the basics in bread production. Simply mix the ingredients together in your table-top mixer using the dough hook for 7 minutes on low speed. If you are a purist, mix together in a large bowl, and then turn the dough out onto a floured surface. Knead with your hands for about 12 minutes. Cover the dough with a damp cloth and let rest for 45 minutes or until the dough doubles in size. Punch down the dough, releasing the gases and cut into four pieces. Roll the dough into logs and place in well oiled loaf pans. On your stovetop, bring a quart of water to a boil. Place the pans in an unheated oven along with the pan of boiling water. Let sit for 45 minutes or until the dough doubles in size again. Remove all items from oven and preheat to 425°. Bake loaves for 20 minutes or until golden brown. Yield: 4 one pound loaves.

Homemade Crackers

7 oz. flour
1/2 tsp. instant yeast
1 Tbsp. olive oil

1/2 tsp. salt
1 Tbsp. honey
4 oz. warm water

Mix together the dry ingredients in a large bowl. Add the honey and the oil. Slowly add the warm water until all is incorporated. Mix by hand for 10 minutes, kneading the dough in the bowl. Turn the dough ball out onto a lightly floured surface and cut into two pieces. Using a rolling pin, flatten each piece until it's about 1/8 to 1/4 inch in thickness and carefully move to a cookie sheet. Brush with water and top with your favorite dry herbs or spices. Lightly tamp down the toppings with the palm of your hand. Bake for 12-15 minutes at 350° or until golden brown. Transfer to cooling rack.

Submitted by: Chef Phil Dreshfield

Blueberry Muffins

Dry Ingredients
8 c. flour
2 tsp. baking soda
3 c. granulated sugar

1 Tbsp. baking powder
2 tsp. salt

Wet Ingredients
1-1/4 c. canola Oil
1 Tbsp. vanilla extract
Zest of 1 lemon

4 eggs, slightly beaten
4 c. buttermilk
2 pts. fresh blueberries

Mix together all the dry ingredients. In a separate bowl, combine all the wet ingredients, except the fruit. Slowly add the wet mixture to the dry ingredients, mixing on low speed until the batter has a consistency of frozen yogurt. Do not over mix. Carefully fold in the fresh berries. Fill paper muffin cups in a muffin pan to 1/4 inch below the rim of the cup. Bake at 350° for 30 minutes or until muffins are golden brown and a toothpick comes out clean from the center. Cool in pan for 30 minutes to allow blueberries to set. Makes 36 muffins.

Whole Wheat Pita Pockets

6 oz. warm water
1 Tbsp. instant yeast
2 Tbsp. honey

1-1/2 tsp. salt
24 oz. bread flour
6 oz. whole wheat flour

Mix the water, yeast, and honey together in a large glass bowl and let rest for five minutes. Once the mixture begins to froth, add the salt and the flours and mix with your hands, kneading the dough for about five minutes. Cover the bowl with a damp cloth and let rest for 30 minutes. Turn out dough on to a lightly floured surface and cut into eight pieces of equal size. Using your hands, roll each piece into a ball. Take each ball, and using a floured rolling pin, flatten the dough until it is about six inches in diameter. Place four pita breads on a cookie sheet and repeat. Bake the two pans of pita in an oven preheated to 425° for about 12 minutes. The pockets will form in the oven. Remove when golden brown

Submitted by: Chef Phil Dreshfield.

Entrees

5 Spice China Grill

2058 S Glenstone Ave
Springfield, MO 65804
417-799-0215

5 Spice China Grill is the first modern Chinese cuisine restaurant in Springfield, MO. Specializing in quality food, with "family style" dining every evening. From the brains of the Tan Brothers that brought Ocean Zen to Springfield, 5 Spice is a fresh new feel to Chinese food. Offering menu items never before seen in this area. Located in the former building of Ocean Zen, acquiring the filling station next door has given additional parking. "Wok Away Specials" are available on some of the menu items for takeout and available through the drive thru. Catering is also available. 5 Spice has a private dining area that accommodates up to 20 people.

Pan Seared Crispy Pork and Shrimp Dumplings with Orange BBQ Sauce

6 oz. ground pork
2 oz. carrots, minced
2 oz. bok choy, minced
3 oz. corn startch
2 oz. oyster sauce

3 oz. rock shrimp, chopped
2 oz. scallions, minced
2 ea. egg whites
3 oz. soy sauce
2 oz. micchu cooking wine

Combine all ingrediants and mix until well incorporated.

Basic dumpling dough:
4 oz. flour

2 oz. warm water

Combine and kneed until dough can stretch about 3 inches.

Orange BBQ sauce:
2 oz. hoison sauce
1 oz. garlic, minced
1 tsp. garlic chile paste
1 oz. orange zest

2 oz. teriyaki sauce
1 oz. ginger, minced
1 tsp. sesame oil

In a sauce pan, combine all ingreients and bring to a boil.

Submitted by: Johnson Tan, Owner & Executive Chef

Andy's Frozen Custard

Springfield
2119 N. Glenstone
3147 E. Sunshine
2726 S. Campbell Ave.
4420 S. Campbell Ave.

Branson
3415 W. Hwy 76

888-60-ANDYS

www.eatandys.com

Andy's has made a science out of frozen custard. We've perfected the method for preparing and serving custard in its highest form, giving you an unparalleled frozen treat. We use the finest ingredients in our mix, a secret recipe of milk, cream, sugar and eggs, which is processed and shipped to Andy's stores within 24 hours to maintain ultimate freshness. Our proprietary frozen custard machines (less than ten are manufactured each year) are customized to Andy's exacting specifications. Andy's Frozen Custard is made fresh hourly and only served at its peak flavor potential of sixty minutes to ensure that our customers get the best frozen custard each time they visit. It's just part of the Andy's difference.

Sauerbraten

2-1/2 c. water
2 onions, finely chopped
1 carrot, sliced
2 juniper berries
1 bay leaf
1 tsp. salt
5 Tbsp. raisins
1 Tbsp. tomato paste
1 tsp. cornstarch

1-1/4 c. wine vinegar
1/2 celery root, chopped
10 peppercorns
2 whole cloves
2-1/4 lbs. beef
1/2 tsp. pepper
3-1/2 oz. butter
1 Tbsp. almonds, chopped

Boil water and vinegar with onions, celery, carrot and spices. Allow to cool and pour over meat in pan. Cover and set aside in cool place for 2-3 days. Turn meat occasionally.

Remove meat from marinade, dry and rub with salt and pepper. Soak raisins in cold water. Heat fat in pan and sear meat on all sides. Strain marinade and sauté vegetables in same pan with meat. Stir in tomato paste and add half of heated marinade. Allow to simmer, covered, for about 2 hours at medium heat. Remove meat and keep warm. Add remaining marinade to broth and stir. Strain and quickly boil again with raisins and almonds. Thicken with cornstarch. Slice meat; serve with gravy and potato dumplings.

Submitted by: Dana & Andy Kuntz, Owners

Argentina Steakhouse

1410 E. Republic road
Springfield, MO 65804
417-886-8010

www.theargentinasteakhouse.com

The Argentina Steakhouse was established in March 2002 in Springfield, Missouri. The family and original staff from Buenos Aries, Argentina opened this independent restaurant in hopes of introducing the people of Springfield to a true steakhouse in the tradition of great cities. As "Springfield's Premiere Steakhouse," the Argentina Steakhouse strives to offer the highest quality and best service to our patrons.

Black Mussels Au Gratin

8 oz. fresh mussels
2 tsp. garlic, minced
1 tsp. fresh parsley, chopped
1/2 tsp. cayenne pepper
4 tsp. butter

1/4 c. onion, sliced
1/4 c. white wine
Salt and pepper to taste
2 tsp. tomato sauce
1 c. Monterey Jack cheese, shredded

In a sauce pan cook the mussels with onion and garlic for two minutes. Add the white wine and season with salt, pepper, cayenne pepper and tomato sauce. Keep cooking on low heat for 2 minutes. After you stir, add the butter and parsley and place it in a baking platter. Add cheese and bake it at 375° for six minutes. Serve with white bread.

Submitted by: Angel Kim, Executive Chef

12) It's All Downtown Trivia

The Roy Blunt Jordan Valley Innovation Center will research:

a. Nanotechnology
b. Biomaterials
c. Genomics/Proteomics
d. All of the above

Answer on page 200

Big Whiskey's American Bar & Grill

311 Park Central E
Springfield, MO 65806
417-862-2449

www.bigwhiskeys.com

Big Whiskey's is all about starting traditions and what better time than our Happy-Hour, Monday through Friday from 4 pm - 6 pm. So come on in and enjoy some of our great half-priced appetizers and take advantage of our 2-for-1 drinks. You will be sure to enjoy our plasma TV's, NTN Trivia, our pool table or maybe some Golden Tee. While you're here, "Submit Your Toast!" Write your favorite toast on a beverage napkin and give to your server or bartender. We pick the best toast once a month. The winner gets a $50 gift card, a Big Whiskey's T-shirt and their toast displayed for a month on our website. So come on in and start a new tradition. Traditions starting daily…

Big Whiskey's Ranch Chicken Alfredo

6 oz. chicken breast, grilled
3/4 c. shredded parmesan
10 oz. cooked penne pasta
2 oz. bacon bits

6 oz. heavy cream
1 Tbsp. ranch seasoning
1/4 c. smoked mozzarella
1 oz. tomatoes, diced

Pour heavy cream into a sauté pan. Set on stove and turn heat to medium. Once cream has started to boil, add the shredded parmesan cheese, bacon bits and ranch mix. Continuously stir until parmesan cheese has fully melted. Add the cooked noodles. Continuously stir until noodles are hot. Cut the chicken into desired amount of slices. Pour pasta into a bowl. Top with chicken, bacon bits, diced tomatoes and smoked mozzarella.

Submitted by: Joshua Hite, Chef

Bijan's Sea & Grille

209 E. Walnut St
Springfield, MO 6580
Phone: 417-831-1480

www.bijans.com

Seared Ahi Tuna with Tabouli Salad and Champagne Vinaigrette

This Ahi tuna recipe is great for summertime because it's not too heavy for those hot summer days.

Champagne Vinaigrette

1/2 c. champagne vinegar
2 Tbsp. whole grain mustard
2 Tbsp. smoked sundried tomatoes
Pinch of salt and pepper
1 Tbsp. Sriracha hot sauce

1 c. champagne
1 Tbsp. roasted garlic
2 Tbsp. fresh parsley
2 Tbsp. honey
1 c. salad oil

Bring all ingredients together in a food processor (except the oil) and mix well. Slowly incorporate the oil into the other ingredients while food processor is mixing. Once the oil is fully incorporated, you will hear the processor start to make a slower or deeper sound. This will let you know when the vinaigrette is finished.

Tabouli Salad:

4 c. water
1 c. fresh parsley, minced
3 ripe tomatoes, diced
Juice of 3 lemons
1/2 Tbsp. all spice
1/2 c. extra virgin olive oil

2 c. Bulgur wheat
1/4 c. mint, minced
1-1/2 cucumbers, diced
1 c. black olives, minced
2 jalapenos, de-seeded and diced
Salt and pepper to taste

Rinse the 2 cups of Bulgur wheat, and then soak in cold water for about 45 minutes. After the 45 minutes, drain off the water and try to dry the wheat as much as possible. Once dried, mix all ingredients together and finally add salt and pepper to taste. When you get this mixture to your liking, cover and chill for an hour before serving.

Pepper Encrusted Tuna:
Take one 8 ounce Ahi Tuna steak and rub with a good amount of cracked black pepper and salt. Almost 50% of the salt and pepper mix will fall off during searing so don't hesitate to put a good crust on the steak. In the sauté pan, use a little extra virgin olive oil and let the pan get fairly hot. The hotter the pan, the better the sear you will get on the tuna. Searing each side of the tuna for about 20 seconds will give you a nice rare temperature for the tuna.

Submitted By: Jeremy Reed, Co-owner

◇◇

Clary's Restaurant

900 E Battlefield Rd
Springfield, MO 65804
417-866-6200

www.eatatclarys.com

The relationship between Farmer, Fisherman and Chef coupled with the evolution of rapid airfreight, has revolutionized the restaurant industry, particularly among fine dining restaurants. At Clary's we now buy produce, poultry, and meat directly from local farmers. We order fish directly from the West coast, Hawaii, and the Gulf of Mexico, and it is flown overnight from the location to your table. We get produce flown to us overnight the day it is picked in California. Our menu now changes regularly to reflect the products we are getting in daily! Our philosophy has not changed, that is, to provide you with the most exciting dining experience possible.

Snapper with Parmesan Crust

4 - 8 oz. filets of snapper   1 c. finely grated parmesan
1/2 c. bread crumbs   1/4 c. olive oil

Make a paste by combining in a food processor the parmesan, bread crumbs, and oil. Top each piece of fish with the crust and bake at 450° for about 15 minutes until fish is just done.

For the sauce:
1 c. dry, white wine   1 Tbsp. shallot, minced
1/4 c. lemon basil pesto   1/2 c. julienne sun-dried tomatoes or vine ripe fresh tomatoes
1 c. heavy cream   Salt and pepper to taste

Combine all ingredients in a medium saucepan and bring to a boil. Let reduce by half. Serve over fish.

Submitted by: James Clary, Owner & Executive Chef

Cooks Kettle Restaurant

At Victory Trade School
200 W. Commercial
Springfield, MO 65803
417-864-2210

www.victorytradeschool.org

Named for Everett and Esther Cook, founders of Springfield Victory Mission, the Cook's Kettle Restaurant provides the culinary laboratory setting for VTS. This restaurant, newly remodeled with a "French Bistro" look, has 2 classically French trained chefs instructing the students as they attend classes in Victory Trade School and receive hands-on training while working various positions in the restaurant. The customers of Cook's Kettle Restaurant agree they return because of the high quality of the food, the low prices, and the cleanliness of the facility. This economical place to eat is a model of how a restaurant can serve good food and practice good hygiene and sanitation. This "student-operated" restaurant provides variety in the menu and all customers are served with professionalism.

Perfect Roasted Poultry

2 c. large carrots, diced
2 c. large stalks celery, diced
8 bay leaves
2 Tbsp. salt
1 turkey, duck, or chicken

2 c. large onions, diced
10 cloves of garlic
1 Tbsp. thyme leaves
1 tsp. black pepper

Season bird inside and out with the salt and pepper. Mix together the diced vegetables, garlic and herbs. Stuff the inside of the bird with the mixture and put the remaining filling in the bottom of the roasting pan. If possible, roast on a rack in the pan to keep it off the bottom. Place 1-2 inches of water in the roasting pan and keep water at that level during baking and cover with foil. Bake at 300-350°, depending on how large your bird is. Chickens, ducks, and small turkeys (9-12 pounds) cook at 350°. Medium turkeys (12-15 pounds) cook at 325°. Large birds at 15 pounds and larger cook at 300°. Most roasting takes about 15 minutes per pound, but allow extra time to rest after cooking. When the bird is 130-150°, take off the foil and allow to brown. Take out of the oven when it is at 180° at the thigh joint with a meat thermometer.

Sautéed Chicken Breast with Raspberry Beaujolais Sauce, Almond Cous Cous, and Wilted Spinach

Sautéed Chicken Breast:

Bone out the breast on two chickens into four separate servings. Season the breast with salt and pepper. Heat a sauté pan until very hot. Put a small amount of oil in the sauté pan. Sauté the chicken breast skin side down until golden brown, turn over and put a small amount of chicken broth in pan, then place in the oven at 350° for 5-8 minutes.

Almond and Scallions Cous Cous:

4 whole green onions, cut on the bias
1/3 c. almonds, toasted
1 Tbsp. olive oil
Salt and white pepper to taste

2-1/2 c. light chicken broth
1-1/3 c. cous cous
4 Tbsp. butter

Bring chicken broth to a boil with the olive oil. Add cous cous and remove from the heat. Cover with a lid. Let stand for at least 5 minutes. Add butter, toasted almonds, salt, pepper, and green onion, then fluff with a fork.

Raspberry Beaujolais Sauce:

1/2 c. Beaujolais wine
1 c. chicken broth
1 Tbsp. corn starch

1 c. fresh raspberries
1/3 c. sugar

Cook wine, raspberries, broth, and sugar for about 5-8 minutes. Strain. Thicken with starch.

Wilted Arugula:

2 Tbsp. olive oil
10 oz. arugula

1 Tbsp. shallot, finely diced
Salt and white pepper to taste

Heat large skillet, add olive oil, and shallots. Add Arugula before the shallots brown. Stir constantly until wilted.

Sautéed Jerk Fish with Banana, Nectarine, and Spiced Rum Sauce

Sauce:

1/2 c. spiced rum
1 clove garlic, minced
1 tsp. lime zest
1 c. orange juice, fresh if you can
2 tsp. sweet Chinese chili sauce or one fresh small, diced jalapeno or hot pepper
2 nectarines, sliced thin

2 Tbsp. butter
1/2 c. brown sugar
Juice from one lime
2 tsp. fresh chopped parsley, just for color
Pinch of salt
2 bananas, sliced thin

Sauté the bananas on medium high in the butter and brown sugar for 2 minutes; put in the nectarines, bring back to boil, then add the rum. Light the rum on fire to burn out alcohol. When rum burns out, add the garlic, chili, lime zest, lime juice, and orange juice. Simmer for a couple minutes until fruit is just soft and mixture becomes a little thicker. Season with salt and add parsley.

Fish:

1 c. flour
1/2 c. oil

2 Tbsp. jerk spice
4 fish filets, some kind of light, white meat fish like snapper, sea bass, sole, or fresh game fish

Mix the jerk spice and flour together, then dust the fish in it. Heat sauté pan until hot, then add the oil to the pan. When oil is hot, add fish and sauté it a few minutes on each side. Make sure to get it golden brown, but do not burn; watch the heat.

Submitted by: Chadwick M Isom, Executive Chef

◇◇

Pecan Crusted Salmon

1/4 c. finely ground pecans
1-1/2 tsp. fresh basil, chopped (or 1/2 tsp. dried)
Non-stick pan spray
4 - 6 oz. salmon fillets

1-1/2 tsp. fresh tarragon, chopped (or 1/2 tsp. dried)
1 Tbsp. olive oil
Pepper to taste

Place pecans, tarragon and basil in food processor; blend in oil. Transfer mixture to a small bowl. Spray baking sheet with non-stick cooking spray and place salmon on baking sheet.

Season with pepper. Spoon equal amounts of pecan herb mixture on each fillet and spread evenly. Bake at 350 ° until cooked through, about 20 minutes. Garnish with lemon slice and parsley or cilantro. Serves 4.

Provides: Calories: 436; Fat: 40.7 gm; Sodium: 96 mg

Salmon, olive oil and pecans are high in total fat but are good sources of omega 3 fatty acids which are protective to the heart.

Submitted by: Cindy Fluekiger RD/LD, Patient Services Coordinator Food & Nutrition Services

Fire & Ice Restaurant and Bar

At Oasis Hotel and Convention Center
2546 N. Glenstone
Springfield, MO 65803
417-522-7711

www.oasisfireandice.com

The Oasis Hotel proudly presents Fire & Ice Restaurant & Bar, where an exquisite atmosphere and culinary creativity welcome hotel guests and the general public. Fire & Ice features Springfield's only curved counter-top ice bar, and offers seating that extends to the indoor pool and its surrounding fountains and plant life, as well as seasonal seating around the hotel's outdoor pool. The open-plan kitchen allows patrons to watch a show of flames behind the ice bar performed by Executive Chef Wing Yee Leong and his team as they prepare the evening's entrees. Dinner fare at Fire & Ice includes seafood delights, steak specialties, and a variety of beef, shrimp, and chicken dishes showcasing Chef Wing's mastery of the wok.

Hoisin Duck on Wonton Crisps with Pineapple Mango Salsa

2 duck breasts or 1/2 roasted duckling
Pineapple mango salsa (see recipe)
Trinity (see recipe)
Hoisin barbecue sauce (see recipe)
4 double-thick wonton skins (if unavailable, use single-thick) or 8 large tortilla chips
Touch of olive oil or chicken broth
1 bunch fresh watercress (if unavailable, substitute with fresh cilantro)
Crème fraiche (substitute with sour cream cut with half & half or milk)

For pineapple mango salsa:

4 oz. pineapple chunks (canned or fresh), diced
1/4 red bell pepper, finely diced
2 oz fresh cilantro, finely diced

2 mangos, diced medium
1/2 onion, finely diced
1/4 c. rice wine vinegar

For the trinity:

1 stalk celery, finely chopped
1/4 red bell pepper, finely chopped

1/4 medium onion, finely chopped

For Hoisin barbecue sauce:

1/2 c. chicken stock
1 Tbsp. oyster sauce
2 Tbsp. rice wine vinegar
1 tsp. sambal olek (Thai chilies)
1/4 tsp. five-spice powder

1 Tbsp. soy sauce
2 Tbsp. Hoisin sauce
1 tsp. fresh garlic, finely chopped
2 Tbsp. sugar

In a bowl, mix together all salsa ingredients until well combined; then set aside. In a small bowl, mix together trinity ingredients until well combined; then set aside. In a bowl, mix together Hoisin barbecue sauce ingredients until well combined; then set aside. Place duck, skin-side down, in a baking pan. Lightly season with salt and pepper and cook in a 325° oven until internal temperature reaches 160°. Remove duck from oven and wait until temperature is comfortable to the touch; then shred or cut into nacho-size pieces and set aside. In a sauté pan over medium heat, sauté the trinity mixture in a scant amount of olive oil or chicken broth for a brief period. Add the shredded duck, then the barbecue sauce and continue to cook until all ingredients are thoroughly warmed. Remove from stove and set aside, keeping warm.

If you prefer wonton skins to pre-packaged large tortilla chips, cut the wonton skins in half to form triangles. Deep fry the triangles and make into chips. Remove from heat, drain and cool.

To serve, arrange eight chips on a plate and divide the duck mixture so that roughly the same amount is placed on each chip. Top the duck mixture on each chip with a dollop of the pineapple mango salsa; drizzle a small amount of crème fraiche over the salsa. Top with small pieces of fresh watercress and serve.

Submitted by: Wing Yee Leong, Executive Chef

13) It's All Downtown Trivia

The number of households within five-miles of Downtown?

a. 44,802   b. 54,601   c. 66,053   d. 72,199

Answer on page 200

First Friday Art Walk

411 N. Sherman Parkway
Springfield, Missouri 65802
417-849-8255

www.ffaw.org

First Friday Art Walk, held 6-10 p.m. the first Friday of each month, is a free walking tour of downtown Springfield's 20-plus art galleries. The event features works by local, regional and national artists, as well as live demonstrations and performances, all in support of First Friday Art Walk's nonprofit mission of promoting fine art and economic vitality in the Downtown Arts District. For more information, give us a call or visit our website.

Pork Loin Chops au Cointreau

4 - 1 inch thick boneless pork loin chops
1/8 c. olive oil
2 Tbsp. fresh ginger, minced
1/2 c. Cointreau or Curacao liqueur
3 Tbsp. powdered chicken stock
2 Tbsp. sour cream
1/2 Tbsp. soy sauce

6-8 medium mushrooms, sliced
1 Tbsp. garlic, minced
6 Tbsp. flour
1/4 Tbsp. cracked pepper
3 Tbsp. Dijon prepared mustard
1 c. whole milk (or more for proper consistency)
1 Tbsp. dried tarragon leaves

Brown pork in oil for about 8 minutes each side and remove. Brown mushrooms in same pan and remove and keep warm with pork while completing sauce. Simmer garlic and ginger in same pan until lightly browned. Add flour to pan and brown, stirring constantly until nutty brown. Add Cointreau (or Curacao) and continue browning. Add rest of ingredients and simmer for few minutes. Put pork and mushrooms back in pan and cover with lid and simmer for about 10-15 minutes. Serves 4.

Submitted by: Sandra CH Smith, Innkeeper & Exec. Director-Springfield Regional Arts Council

Gallery Bistro

221 E Walnut St
Springfield, MO 65806
417-866-0555

www.gallerybistrodowntown.com

Gallery
Bistro

Gallery Bistro is located on Historic Walnut Street in Downtown Springfield; just two doors down from the Landers Theatre and next to the Vandivort Theatre. Our contemporary cuisine is an eclectic mix of Asian, French, English, Spanish and Down-home. Friendly, attentive and knowledgeable service is our trademark. Combined with our extensive wine collection and massive martini repertoire, our patrons are ensured of a fabulous dining experience. Gallery Bistro is the place to go for dinner or light fare before the show, or after the curtain falls. Late night cocktails and an appetizer - or our famous mushroom sage soup - are favorites of Springfield theater-goers.

Grilled Ahi Tuna with Seafood Kabob and Mediterranean Salsa, with Goat Cheese Polenta Cake and Fresh Asparagus

4 - 8 oz. Ahi tuna steaks
3 Tbsp. olive oil
Salt and pepper
8 large shrimp
1 c. Italian polenta (corn meal)
1 oz. goat cheese
Salt and pepper
1 Tbsp. olive oil

1 Tbsp. fresh rosemary
Juice of one lemon
4 large sea scallops
4 bamboo skewers
3 c. water
1 tsp. finely chopped mixed herbs
20 asparagus spears
Salt and pepper

Salsa:

3 ripe roma tomatoes, diced
1/2 red onion, chopped
1 tsp. fresh basil, chopped
Juice of 2 lemons

1 Tbsp. capers
2 cloves garlic, chopped
1/4 c. extra virgin olive oil
Salt and pepper

Prepare the salsa by combining all the ingredients together. Place in a covered container in the refrigerator for at least an hour.

Polenta:

Bring the water to a boil in a heavy sauce pot with salt and pepper. When boiling, whisk the polenta in, stirring continuously. Reduce the heat and allow the polenta to cook slowly for 5 minutes. When the polenta is thick, remove from heat and stir in the goat cheese and herbs. Check seasoning and adjust if necessary. Pour the polenta into a small baking pan, cool, and transfer to the refrigerator for 2 hours or until firm. Remove the pan of polenta and turn it out onto a clean cutting board. Cut into desired sized cakes. When the grill is hot, brush the polenta cakes with a little oil and place them on the grill. Allow them to cook for 4-7 minutes on each side, then remove and keep warm.

Asparagus:

On a baking sheet, lay the asparagus out flat and brush with olive oil and sprinkle with salt and pepper. Clean the grill and transfer the asparagus to the grill. Cook for about 4 minutes; then remove and keep warm.

Thread the shrimp and scallops onto the bamboo skewers. On a separate baking sheet mix the olive oil, lemon juice, rosemary, salt and pepper. Dip each side of the tuna in this mix and each of the seafood kabobs; cover and return the tuna and kabobs to the refrigerator. Clean the grill and place the kabobs on. Place the tuna steaks on. Cook the kabobs until the shrimp are no longer translucent, about 3 minutes on each side. Turn the tuna steaks, cooking about 2-3 minutes on each side to achieve a rare center.

Arrange the warm polenta cakes, asparagus, tuna steaks and kabobs on 4 plates and dress with the salsa. Serve immediately. Serves 4.

Submitted by: Peter Tinson, Owner & Executive Chef

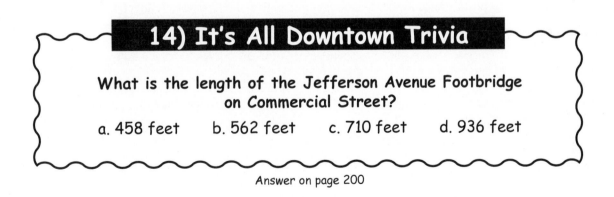

14) It's All Downtown Trivia

What is the length of the Jefferson Avenue Footbridge on Commercial Street?

a. 458 feet   b. 562 feet   c. 710 feet   d. 936 feet

Answer on page 200

Gary Fenton, CPA, P.C.

The Vandivort Center
305 E. Walnut, Ste 105
Springfield, MO 65806
417-865-2323

gary@fentoncpa.com

Mojo Marinated Pork with Dipping Sauce

4-1/2 c. fresh orange juice
1 orange, zested
1/2 c. fresh oregano, finely chopped
1/2 c. olive oil
Salt and freshly ground black pepper

1-1/4 c. fresh lime juice
1 lime, zested
12 cloves garlic, coarsely chopped
1 bone-in pork shoulder (about 4-6 lbs.), trimmed of excess fat
Mojo Dipping Sauce (recipe follows)

Combine 4 cups of the orange juice and 1 cup of the lime juice and zest in a large saucepan over high heat and reduce to 2 cups. Remove from the heat and stir in the remaining orange juice and lime juice; add a few cloves of garlic and 1/4 cup of the oregano. Let cool to room temperature. Using a paring knife, make small slits over the entire surface of the pork and rub the garlic into the slashes. Whisk together the oil and remaining 1/4 cup of the oregano in a large roasting pan; add the pork and turn to coat. Cover and let marinate in the refrigerator for at least 4 hours and up to 24 hours. Preheat the oven to 425° F. Remove the pork from the refrigerator 30 minutes before roasting. Season the pork with salt and pepper and cook for 30 minutes. Reduce the heat to 375° F. and continue roasting, basting with the marinade during the last 30 minutes of roasting until golden brown and an instant-read thermometer inserted into the center reaches 150° F. Remove from the oven, baste with any remaining glaze, tent loosely and let rest 15 minutes before slicing.

Dipping Sauce:

8 cloves garlic
3 Tbsp. chopped cilantro leaves
1/2 c. orange juice
1/4 c. extra virgin olive oil

1 Serrano chili, chopped
Salt to taste
1/4 c. lime juice

Using a mortar and pestle, mash the garlic, Serrano chilies, cilantro and a few pinches of salt until it becomes a paste. Add the orange juice, lime juice and oil and stir to combine.

Submitted by: Gary Fenton, CPA, P. C.

Gem of India
Restaurant & Bar

211 W. Battlefield
Springfield, MO 65807
417-881-9558

www.gemofindia.net

Gem of India has been serving Springfield with fine Indian cuisine for many years. The chef/owner has worked in fine Indian restaurants in Boston since 1992. We serve authentic Indian cuisine made with the finest and freshest ingredients. We strive to provide excellent service and mouth-watering delicacies with an enticing ambience. We hope to serve Springfield for a long time to come.

Butter Chicken

1/4 pt. plain yogurt	2 oz. ground almonds
1-1/2 tsp. chili powder	1/4 tsp. crushed bay leaves
1/4 tsp. ground cloves	1/4 tsp. ground cinnamon
1 tsp. garam masala	4 green cardamom pods
1 tsp. ginger pulp	1 tsp. garlic pulp
14 oz. can tomatoes	1-1/4 tsp. salt
2 lbs. chicken, skinned, boned and cubed	3 oz. butter
1 Tbsp. corn oil	2 medium onions, sliced
2 Tbsp. fresh coriander, chopped	4 Tbsp. cream

Place the yogurt, ground almonds, all the dry spices, ginger, garlic, tomatoes and salt in a mixing bowl and blend together thoroughly. Put the chicken into a large mixing bowl and pour over the yogurt mixture. Set aside. Melt together the butter and oil in a medium karahi, (pan) wok or frying pan. Add the onions and fry for about 3 minutes. Add the chicken mixture and stir-fry for about 7 to 10 minutes. Stir in about half of the coriander and mix well. Pour over the cream and stir in well. Bring to a boil. Garnish the Indian butter chicken with the remaining chopped coriander to serve the chicken curry.

Submitted by: Singh Gurdev, Owner

Hemingway's Blue Water Cafe

Located on the 4th floor of Bass Pro Shops
1935 S Campbell
Springfield, MO 65898
417-891-5100

www.hemingwaysbluewatercafe.com

Hemingway's Blue Water Café is a fantastic place to eat for any occasion. We have a variety of entrees for an unforgettable meal. We provide a fun dining experience in a unique casual atmosphere showcasing a 30,000 gallon saltwater tank and numerous exotic displays. Our menu features a wide variety of selections from hand cut steaks and half pound burgers to Ahi tuna and our chicken Caesar sandwich on grilled flatbread. In addition to our high quality menu items, we offer a buffet for breakfast, lunch and dinner, Monday through Saturday as well as a brunch buffet on Sunday. A kids menu is available and children 4 and under eat free off of the daily buffets.

Shrimp Tequila

6 - 21/25 shrimp, butter flied, peeled and deveined
1 Tbsp. shallots, finely diced
1/2 oz. pimentos, drained and diced
1/2 tsp. cilantro
2 oz. heavy cream
5 oz. angel hair pasta, cooked
Flour to dredge

1 oz. butter
1/2 oz. mushrooms, sliced
1/8 tsp. garlic, chopped
1 oz. tequila
6 oz. tequila lime sauce
1 Tbsp. parsley, chopped

In sauté pan heat butter, dredge shrimp in flour and sauté. Remove shrimp and keep warm. To skillet add shallots, mushrooms, pimentos and sauté until soft. Add garlic and cilantro and deglaze with tequila. Add cream and bring to a boil, add tequila lime sauce and parsley; simmer 1 minute. Serve over bed of angel hair pasta and garnish with parsley.

Submitted by: Marcel Bonetti, CEC, AAC, Executive Chef

Honey Heaven & the Vineyard Tea Room

2516 S Campbell
Springfield, MO 65807
417-869-0233

www.honeyheaven.com

Honey Tarragon Salmon

8 salmon fillets
1/4 c. lemon juice
1 Tbsp. tarragon
1/4 tsp. salt

1/2 c. olive oil
2 Tbsp. water
1 Tbsp. Honey Heaven's Golden, Glorious & Pure Honey

Mix all ingredients together in a measuring cup; pour over salmon or fish of choice in either frozen or thawed state. Marinate for at least 15 minutes before grilling/broiling. Brush with marinade sauce over the fish. Cook fish 8-10 minutes per side. Fish will flake when done.
Serves 4-6.

Submitted by: Lena Meyer, "The Honey Lady"

Maria's Mexican Restaurant

406 South Ave,
Springfield, MO 65806
831-9339

Maria's Mexican Restaurant was one of the first businesses to help revitalize downtown Springfield. A family owned restaurant, we began in a small take-out spot on Walnut Street in 1997. Thanks to our loyal clientele we were able to move to a larger location on South Ave in 2001. We offer full service dine-in with take-out still available, a full bar with over 160 varieties of tequila. Catering available for any event.

Chicken, Black Bean and Cheddar Cheese Tamales

1/2 lb. dried corn husk
1 tsp. salt
1 c. vegetable oil
12 oz black beans, rinsed and drained

2 c. masa harina (can be found at local stores)
2 to 2-1/2 c. warm chicken broth
2-1/2 c. shredded chicken
12 oz. cheddar cheese

Soak corn husk in hot water till soft, about 30 minutes. Be sure to remove any corn silk.

Filling:
Combine chicken, black beans and cheese; set aside.

Masa:
Combine masa, salt and oil. Add broth in increments of 1/2 cup, mixing well. It's best to use your hands to mix the dough. The dough is the desired consistency if it is dry enough to hold together, yet moist enough to spread easily.

Remove corn husk from water, drain excess water. Hold husk in palm of hand or lay on flat work surface; starting about 1/4 of the way down from pointed end, spread 2 Tablespoons of masa over the husk. Place about 3 ounces of filling in the center of masa. Fold sides to center so they overlap, then fold top of husk down to rest on seam.

Stand tamales upright in a steamer starting from the center and working outward. Do not pack the tamales too tight. Fill any empty spaces with extra husk or foil. Add water cover and cook on a low flame for about 50 minutes. Check water level periodically. Tamales are done when they separate easily from the husk. Top with salsa, pico de gallo, cheese or your favorite hot sauce.

Submitted by: Monica Guest, Co-owner

Metro Builders Supply

3252 N Glenstone
Springfield MO 65803
417-833-1113

www.metrobuilderssupply.com

METRO BUILDERS SUPPLY
"Your Home Appliance Specialist"

Metro Builders Supply is the largest appliance distributor in the Midwest. With nine stores in four states, Metro has the buying power to offer the lowest possible price on more than 30 brands of major appliances. Whether you are a builder, contractor, or homeowner, Metro has the product to meet your needs and your budget. Each of our locations provides an extensive display of products, many showcased in kitchen cabinetry. Our employee-owned company prides itself with expert salespeople who offer years of appliance sales experience and extraordinary customer service. Our showroom in Springfield, MO offers an extensive lighting department as well. The largest selection, the lowest prices... experience Metro!

Autumn Pork Chops

1 Tbsp. vegetable oil
1 can condensed cream of celery soup
2 Tbsp. spicy brown mustard
Hot cooked medium egg noodles

4 pork chops (1/2 inch thick)
1/2 c. apple juice
1 Tbsp. honey
1/4 tsp. pepper

Heat oil in large skillet over medium-high heat. Cook pork chops for 10 minutes until browned on both sides. Add soup, apple juice, mustard, honey and pepper. Bring to a boil. Cover and cook over low heat 5 minutes or until chops are done. Serve over warm noodles.

Grilled Pesto Chicken Packets

*Great for outdoor grilling with friends. Make the packets in advance and spend time
visiting with friends while they cook.*

4 boneless skinless chicken breast halves (1 1/4 lbs.)
4 small zucchini, cut into 1/2 inch slices

8 Roma tomatoes, cut into 1/2 inch slices
1/2 c. basil pesto

Heat coals or gas grill for direct heat. Place 1 chicken breast half, 2 slices of tomato and 1 slice of zucchini on one side of four 18 x 12 inch sheets of heavy duty aluminum foil. Spoon 2 tablespoons pesto over chicken mixture on each sheet. Fold foil over chicken and vegetables so edges meet. Seal edges making tight 1/2 inch fold; fold again. Allow space on sides for circulation and expansion. Cover and grill packets 4-5 inches from medium heat 20-25 minutes or until juice of chicken is no longer pink. Place packets on plates. Cut large X across top of packet; fold back foil. Yield: 4 servings.

Submitted By: Judy Bilyeu, Metro Builders Supply

Metropolitan Grill

2931 East Battlefield
Springfield, MO 65804
417-889-4951

www.metropolitan-grill.com

Metropolitan Grill is the "Cheers" of fine dining. Where Spain meets Italy in the heart of the Ozarks. I love people, and I love to cook, so the restaurant is my vehicle to achieve what I love. Relax and let the atmosphere and a great glass of wine fill your senses while we create unique dishes for you in our display kitchen. My Cooking Philosophy: 'Creation.' As an Executive Chef I challenge my kitchen staff every day to 'create, not copy'. Many artists can paint Picasso; many pianists can play Mozart; and yes, many Chefs can make Emeril's dishes. My menu is inspired by my restaurant family and my emotions. Enjoy our "creations."

Ethridge Salmon

2 - 8 oz. salmon fillets
2 Tbsp. unsalted butter
1/2 c. pear juice
2 pieces cooked bacon, chopped
1/4 c. heavy whipping cream

Home-made chicken stock
1 Tbsp. cracked black pepper
1/2 c. white wine
3 sprigs fresh tarragon

Home-made chicken stock:
Bring 1 cup chicken broth (brand of your choice) and 1/4 cup white wine to a boil. Mix 3 cups cold tap water and 1/2 cup cornstarch; whisk together. Add more cornstarch, if necessary, until you have a slightly thick paste.

Add 5 ounces chicken stock, pear juice, butter, cracked black pepper and white wine in 10 inch sauté pan. Place both salmon fillets skin side down in pan. Bring to a boil. Once salmon begins to turn pale, flip. Remove skins. Add bacon and tarragon. Continue to flip salmon from side to side until desired temperature is reached. Stir in heavy whipping cream to finish. Serves 2.

Submitted by: Pat Duran, Owner & Executive Chef

Mille's Café

313 S Jefferson Ave
Springfield, MO 65806
(417) 831-1996

www.millescafe.com

August of 1999, Mille's Turn of The Century Café opened on Jefferson in Historic Downtown Springfield. An Urban Casual Café, Mille's brought unique, yet affordable dining to downtown.

Open for lunch and dinner, Mille's truly has something for everyone. With over 100 items on the menu, a full bar and wine list, four private dining/meeting rooms, outside seating and a 225 person Banquet room that is perfect for weddings, class reunions or a surprise get together.

Apple Walnut Pork Tenderloin

2 - 1 to 1-1/2 lb. pork tenderloins
1/2 c. honey
Dash of Worcestershire sauce
1 tsp. granulated garlic
1 lunchbox portion of applesauce
1/4 c. sugar

1 c. soy sauce
1 tsp. ground ginger
2 c. hot tap water
1 stick butter (soft)
1/4 c. walnuts
1 tsp. cinnamon

Remove all fat and silver skin from your tenderloins; some butchers will do this for you at time of purchase. Butterfly the tenderloin down the length of it, and then cut them in half. Set aside.

Marinade:
Dissolve honey in hot tap water, then add soy sauce, ginger, Worcestershire and granulated garlic. Pour over pork tenderloin portions.

Apple Walnut Butter:
Place butter, walnuts, applesauce, cinnamon and sugar in a mixer. Beat on high till well whipped and evenly blended. Set aside.

Grill, broil, or bake pork tenderloins to desired doneness. When done and ready to serve, put a golf ball size dollop of butter on top of pork tenderloin and let it melt over the pork. Serve with a nice vegetable and rice pilaf and enjoy!!

Submitted by: David Bauer, Mille's Turn of the Century Café

Nonna's Italian American Café

306 South Ave
Springfield, MO 65806
417-831-1222

www.nonnascafe.com

Funky, Fun, Eclectic, and Relaxed, Nonna's Italian American Café has been a downtown classic for over 12 years. Delicious Food, Homemade Desserts, Friendly Prices and a Full Bar. Featuring Full-Service Catering, Event Planning, A Jazz Guitarist Duo on Thursday Night, A Classical Guitarist on Friday Night, A Jazz Guitarist on Saturday Night, A Musical Theatre Open-Mic Sunday Night called 'The Cast Party,' Monthly Operazzi Nights, and Monthly Art Shows. Join us for the First Friday Art Walk. Open Daily. Locally World Famous.

Cavatelli Carbonara

Per Person:

2 oz. small pancetta, diced
1 egg (beaten)
1 tsp. coarse cracked pepper
1 oz. parsley and green onion, chopped
Cooking oil

1 Tbsp. Dijon mustard
6 oz. heavy cream
8 oz. cooked cavatelli pasta
Salt and white pepper to taste

In a pre-heated pan, put a small amount of cooking oil and the pancetta. Cook until the pancetta is crisp. Add heavy cream and Dijon, and stir/mix until the mustard is fully incorporated into the cream. Let stand until you get a rolling boil with the cream mixture. Add the pasta and cracked pepper and toss or stir. Slowly add the egg into the pan while constantly mixing. The sauce will tighten as the egg cooks in the mixture. Finally, add in chopped parsley and onion and toss. The consistency should be creamy but not loose.

Penne al Arrabbiata

4 oz. vodka
2 c. stewed tomatoes
Salt and white pepper to taste
1/2 c. parmesan cheese

12 oz. heavy cream
2 tsp. crushed red pepper
1 lb. penne pasta

Pasta:

In a pot of boiling water with a pinch of salt, add the dry pasta and stir. Let the pasta boil for approximately 8 minutes or until done; strain and put aside.

Sauce:

In a saucepan over high heat, add the tomatoes, vodka and crushed red pepper; reduce the liquid, thus burning out the alcohol from the vodka. Add in the cream, letting it get to a rolling boil. Put in the pasta and stir/toss. Add in the parmesan cheese until fully incorporated.

Options:

Add grilled chicken breast or any other meat or seafood that you desire. Serves 4 - 8 people

Submitted by: Martin P Almaraz, Co-owner

Pappy's Place

943 N. Main Avenue
Springfield, MO 65802
417-866-8744

Pappy's Place has stood at this location since 1904. While now housing a bar/restaurant, the store first began as a family-owned shoe repair shop. Shortly after that, the owners opened a grocery store and kept it that way until the 1920s. New owners opened a cafe on the property in 1924. Following Prohibition, the cafe applied for a beer-by-the-drink license. This license, which is still held by Pappy's, is the oldest continuous license in Springfield. Pappy's Place may be old, and not very well-known, but it is a place of character. The people are friendly, the food is good and the beer is cold. A casual atmosphere makes for a laid-back time. For many people, it is a place of good memories.

Shrimp Madeleine

12 large shrimp
2 Tbsp. green onions, chopped
1 stalk celery, chopped
3 cloves garlic, chopped
Dash hot pepper flakes

1/2 stick butter, unsalted
1/2 green bell pepper, chopped
2 Tbsp. lemon juice
Dash Worcestershire
Grilled French bread (coated with olive oil)

Sauté ingredients, except the shrimp for about 3 minutes. Add the shrimp and cook for another 5 minutes. Serve with grilled French bread as a garnish.

Submitted by: Jack Rauhoff, Chef

Peabody's

312 E. Commercial St
Springfield, Mo. 65803
417-832-8585

Pan-Seared Tuna with Cilantro Lime Sauce

4 – 6-8 oz. Yellow Fin Tuna steaks   2 Tbsp. olive oil

Sear tuna in a large skillet – turning once to temperature - rare, med, or well done.
(We love it Rare!)

Cilantro Lime Sauce:
1 c. heavy whipping cream   1/8 c. sweet lime mixer
1 Tbsp. dried cilantro (Dried works better than fresh in this sauce)

Over low heat, cook cream until barely simmering. Add lime mixer and cilantro. Cook until reduced to a thick sauce. Pour sauce over tuna steaks and garnish with red bell pepper strips and a thin slice of lime.

Submitted by: Ron Peabody, Owner

Ocean Zen Pacific Rim

600 E Battlefield St
Springfield, MO 65807
417-889-9596

www.eatoceanzen.com

Springfield's premiere Pacific Rim restaurant, Ocean Zen has brought the fusion of East meets west to the Ozarks. Featuring many culinary delights including sushi. The Tan Brothers (John and Chef Johnson Tan) opened in November of 2004. In the spring of 2007 they expanded to a larger building located at 600 East Battlefield. Saving the atmosphere people have grown to love, the new building offers a larger bar area, three banquet rooms to accommodate larger parties and dining. Open for lunch seven days a week from 11am-3pm. Dinners start at 4:30pm to close. Ocean Zen offers a drive thru, as well as catering options.

Apple Wood Bacon Wrapped Seared Rare Hawaiian Ono "Wahoo" With Malaysian Style Spicy Warm Curry Potato Salad and Creamy Lemon Basil Vinaigrette

2 strips apple wood bacon
Salt to taste

5 oz. Hawaiian Ono "Wahoo"
Cracked black pepper

Wrap the Ono with the bacon; season with salt and crust with black pepper. In a sauté pan, heat olive oil and sear the fish to rare or medium rare.

Malaysian Curry Potato Salad:

6 oz. red bliss potatoes, diced
2 oz. red onion, diced
1 tsp. chili garlic sauce
1 tsp. Madras curry powder

3 oz. trio bell peppers, diced
2 oz. mayonnaise
1 oz. sugar
1 oz. chopped cilantro

Fry potatoes until done and combine all ingredients and mix well.

Creamy Lemon Basil Dressing:

4 oz. heavy cream
Juice of half a lemon
1 oz. basil, chopped

2 oz. olive oil
Salt and white pepper to taste

Combine all ingredients together and emulsify with olive oil.

Mongolian Glazed Lamb Chops with Wasabi Mashed Potatoes and Thai Coconut Curry Basil Sauce

3 ea. - 3 oz. lamb chops
Salt and pepper to taste

4 oz. Wasabi mashed potatoes (see recipe below)
Mongolian BBQ sauce (see recipe below)

Grill lamb chops to your liking; glaze with Mongolian BBQ sauce.

Mongolian BBQ sauce:

2 oz. hoison sauce
1 oz. ginger and garlic, minced

1 oz. teriyaki sauce

Combine all ingredients together and mix.

Wasabi mashed potatoes:

6 oz. steamed potatoes
4 oz. spinach puree
Salt and pepper to taste

1 oz. Wasabi paste
1 c. heavy cream
4 oz. butter

Combine all ingredients together and mix with a whisk until nice and smooth.

Thai coconut curry basil sauce:

1 can coconut milk
1 oz. garlic, minced
2 oz. sugar
2 oz. fish sauce

2 oz. lemongrass stalks
1 oz. ginger, minced
4 oz. green curry paste
2 oz. cilantro

Sauté lemongrass, garlic, ginger and curry paste. Deglaze the pan with fish sauce and add coconut milk, sugar and cilantro; reduce by half.

Tri Pepper Seared Rare Ahi Tuna with Enoki Mushrooms, Tobiko Caviar and Lobster Cognac Bisque

4 oz. Hawaiian Yellow Fin Ahi Tuna
1 oz. Tobiko caviar
Garnish chopped chives
Season kosher salt

2 oz. Enoki mushrooms
1 oz. pink ginger
2 oz. ground peppercorns

Crust the tuna with the salt and peppercorns. In a sauté pan, sear the tuna with olive oil until rare consistency, 10 seconds on each side. Slice the tuna into 1/4 inch pieces and plate up with the sauce. Garnish with Enoki mushrooms, pink ginger, chives and Tobiko caviar.

Sauce:

1 ea. Maine lobster body
1 oz. garlic, minced
2 oz. cognac
4 oz. carrots
2 qt. heavy cream

6 oz. shrimp shells
2 oz. tomato paste
4 oz. onions
2 oz. celery
1 c. tomato, chopped

Sauté onions, carrots, celery and garlic. Add lobster body and shrimp shells; cook until shells turn red color. Add tomato paste, chopped tomatoes, cognac and heavy cream. Reduce by half and blend in blender until smooth.

Submitted by: Johnson Tan, Owner & Executive Chef

Riad Mediterranean Cuisine

105 Park Central Square
Springfield, MO 65806
417-866-1151

1250 E. Republic
Springfield, MO 65806
417-881-RIAD (7423)

www.riadcuisine.com

Since opening in February of 2004, Riad cuisine has proudly given the Springfield area a taste of the Mediterranean. With the health conscious menu, customers can enjoy a tasty meal without guilt. Meeting rooms are available at both locations. Our private rooms are conveniently located and tastefully decorated with various seating arrangements that can accommodate your needs. Ideal for meetings, parties, receptions, conferences, or retreats. Optional services include complete meals, catering, high speed internet, projection screen, TV with cable and bar service. Call to reserve.

Dejage

1 lb. chicken breast
2 c. white long grain rice
2 c. yellow onion, chopped
2 c. broccoli, chopped

4-1/2 c. water
2 Tbsp. olive oil
2 Tbsp. water
8 cloves garlic, minced

Cut chicken breast into small cubes, removing fat. Boil 4-1/2 cups of water in a medium size pot. Once water is at rapid boil, add rice, reducing heat to medium and covering with a tight fitting lid. Cook rice at medium for 10 minutes; do not stir rice while it is cooking. While rice is cooking, heat 2 tablespoons of olive oil in a large skillet at medium-high. Add chicken breast and cook for 2 minutes. Add 2 cups of onion and sauté both until chicken is cooked throughout, about 7-10 minutes. Add 2 tablespoons of water, 2 cups of broccoli and minced garlic. Sauté for 2 minutes or till broccoli is soft. Once completed, serve dejage on a bed of rice. Serves 4.

Submitted by: Riad Matar, Owner

Rodizio Brazilian Grill

3371 E Montclair St
Springfield, MO 65804
417-881-8882

www.springfieldrodizio.com

Whether an intimate dinner for two, an employee lunch for 10 or a business meeting and meal for 50, our Brazilian Steak House is the perfect place. Our fixed-price menu includes Brazilian Cheese bread and appetizers, the cold bar, and all 18 selections of beef, pork, lamb and poultry. You enjoy as much as you want and when you want it - with our unique Rodizio-style service. Our elegant yet fun atmosphere along with private and customized dining areas will accommodate almost any need. We are proud to share with you our food, traditions and culture ~ all in a beautiful setting. We invite you to explore our web site and learn more about our authentic Churrascaria (shoo-rah-scah-REE-ah) style of dining.

Pot-Roasted Duck and Green Vegetables

8 oz. duck breast
2 tsp. leeks, sliced
1 c. broccoli
1 tsp. lime juice

1/4 c. shitake mushrooms, sliced
2 tsp. Belgian endives, chopped
1 c. baby spinach
Salt and pepper to taste

In a saucepan cook the duck breast on the skin side first for three minutes. The duck breast will release oil that should be put on the side. Cook the other side of the duck for three minutes. Bake the breast in 375° for 5 minutes. In the mean time, pour the oil set aside earlier into another pan and cook all the vegetables for 5 minutes, stirring constantly. Add the sake and seasoning to the vegetables and place the duck breast into the pan and let simmer for 3-4 minutes before serving.

Submitted by: Angel Kim, Executive Chef

Springfield Brewing Company

305 South Market St
Springfield, MO 65806
417-832-TAPS (8277)

www.springfieldbrewingco.com

Springfield Brewing Company was established in 1997. As the most unique dining experience in Springfield, we feature an expansive menu, award winning hand-crafted ales and lagers, banquet facilities, outdoor dining, pool tables and live music Wednesday through Sunday. We invite you down to help us celebrate our 10 year anniversary and the opening of the College Station car park.

Almond Chicken

2 oz. margarine
1/4 c. flour seasoned with pepper and salt
2 oz. white wine
2 oz. butter, unsalted

1 - 6 oz. marinated chicken breast
1 oz. sliced almonds, untoasted
3 oz. amaretto

Dust chicken breast with flour mixture. Sauté chicken in melted margarine until cooked throughout. Deglaze the sauté pan with white wine to release the chicken. Add sliced almonds to the top of chicken. Add amaretto to pan. Once amaretto is boiling, add unsalted butter and swirl until mixture is thickened.

Submitted by: Kevin Mackey, Owner

Tower Club

The Hammons Tower
901 E Saint Louis St # 2100
Springfield, MO 65806
(417) 866-4466

www.towerclubspringfield.com

Main Dining room hours: Tuesday through Friday, 11 a.m. - 2 p.m. Top of the Tower Dining Room: Tuesday through Thursday, 5 p.m. - 9 p.m. Friday and Saturday, 5 p.m. - 10 p.m. Closed on Sundays and Mondays
The Club will accommodate private parties during regular hours of operation. Special arrangements may be made for parties outside of normal Club hours with Club Manager.
Amenities: Finest food and service. Exquisite dining room and lounge. Panoramic view of the city. Special promotions. Five private suites seat up to 30. Starlight Room accommodates up to 150 people. Reciprocity at over 150 clubs throughout the world.
A Gentle Reminder: Please make reservations for lunch and dinner before coming to The Club. It helps us serve you better.

Chicken Diane

2 - 7 oz. chicken breasts (cut in half and pounded flat)
1-1/2 oz. olive oil
3 Tbsp. shallots
1/2 c. red wine
1/2 c. cream
3/4 c. brown sauce

3 Tbsp. seasoned flour
2 Tbsp. Dijon mustard
2 c. mushrooms, sliced
1 Tbsp. Worcestershire sauce

Roll chicken in seasoned flour. In medium size skillet, sauté chicken in olive oil on medium heat. When chicken begins to brown, turn and brown the other side. Brush chicken with mustard. Add shallots and mushrooms and cook until mushrooms and shallots are tender. Turn heat to high and add red wine and reduce by half. Add cream and Worcestershire. When cream begins to thicken, add brown sauce and turn to low heat. Let simmer for 2 minutes. Serves 2.

Submitted by: Brad Lyons, C.E.C. Executive Chef

Taste of Springfield

Sides/Misc.

1955 Maple Cafe

2253 N Glenstone Ave
Springfield, MO 65803
417-865-5656

1955 MAPLE CAFE

HOME OF THE $2.99 BREAKFAST SPECIAL – 2 EGGS, BACON, TOAST AND COFFEE

The 1955 Maple Cafe was established in 1955 just as the namesake indicates. It was built along historic Route 66 and is part of Springfield history. The new owners took over in 2007 and pride themselves on running a Christian-based establishment, with cookin' just the way mom made it. They have daily specials and a great hometown atmosphere. The customers are called family; well because they pretty much live there!

Deep South Crock-Pot Mac and Cheese

1 - 16 oz. box of macaroni
2 sticks butter
2 c. milk

6 c. shredded sharp cheese
2 cans evaporated milk
2 eggs

In a large saucepan, cook and drain macaroni. Melt butter in the hot macaroni. Remove from heat. Add 4-1/2 cups of cheese, evaporated milk, and milk. Beat eggs lightly and add to mixture. Lightly spray your crock pot with cooking spray. Add mixture to a large crock pot, top with remaining 1-1/2 cups of cheese. Cook 3 hours on low setting or 2 hours on high setting. (This recipe can be cut in half and added to a smaller crock pot.)

Mayonnaise Muffins

1-1/2 c. self-rising flour
1/4 c. mayonnaise
Add milk or buttermilk to create a thick pancake-like batter

Preheat oven to 425°. Grease muffin pan and pour batter into pan. Makes 6 muffins. Bake for 30 minutes.

Submitted by: Hollie Davis, Owner

Andy's Frozen Custard

Springfield
2119 N. Glenstone
3147 E. Sunshine
2726 S. Campbell Ave.
4420 S. Campbell Ave.

Branson
3415 W. Hwy 76

888-60-ANDYS

www.eatandys.com

Andy's has made a science out of frozen custard. We've perfected the method for preparing and serving custard in its highest form, giving you an unparalleled frozen treat. We use the finest ingredients in our mix, a secret recipe of milk, cream, sugar and eggs, which is processed and shipped to Andy's stores within 24 hours to maintain ultimate freshness. Our proprietary frozen custard machines (less than ten are manufactured each year) are customized to Andy's exacting specifications. Andy's Frozen Custard is made fresh hourly and only served at its peak flavor potential of sixty minutes to ensure that our customers get the best frozen custard each time they visit. It's just part of the Andy's difference.

Red Cabbage (easy way)

2 Tbsp. brown sugar
1 Tbsp. oil (or bacon fat)
2 Tbsp. water
Dash pepper
3/4 c. apple, coarsely chopped
1 bay leaf

2 Tbsp. vinegar
1/2 tsp. caraway seed
1/2 tsp. salt
2 c. shredded red cabbage
3 whole cloves

In large skillet, stir together first 7 ingredients. Cook 2-3 min. or until hot, stirring occasionally. Stir in cabbage and apple. Cook, covered, over medium-low heat for 10-12 minutes or until crisp-tender. Stir occasionally while cooking.

Submitted by: Dana & Andy Kuntz, Owners

Avanzare Italian Dining

1908 S. Glenstone
Springfield, MO 65804
417-567-3463

www.avanzareitaliandining.com

Exceptional Northern Italian cuisine is the center piece of Avanzare. As you dine with us, you'll find world class chef Tony Garcia prepares each dish with only the finest freshly sourced ingredients, including fresh made bread and desserts. A little bit of Italy sits quietly "On the Plaza at Glenstone and Sunshine." Surrounding ourselves with only the best ensures your dining experience at Avanzare is what you anticipate and deserve!

Bistecca Rosemarino

2 - 14 oz. ribeye
1 yellow squash
1 tsp. garlic, chopped
2 oz. of dry white wine
Salt and black pepper
1 Tbsp. olive oil

1 zucchini
1/3 c. heavy cream
1 tsp. fresh rosemary, chopped
1 Tbsp. gorgonzola cheese
1 Tbsp. butter

Process:
Season the ribeye with salt, black pepper and rosemary. Pan sear in a hot skillet for five minutes on each side, cook to desired temperature.

Vegetables:
Slice the zucchinis and yellow squash--- in thick medallions and sauté in a hot skillet with a little olive oil and salt and pepper to taste.

Sauce:
In a medium hot skillet, add olive oil and garlic; let the garlic turn to a golden brown. Then add the white wine and let it cook to reduction for a couple minutes. Add the heavy cream and cook for 2 to 3 minutes; add the gorgonzola cheese, butter, salt and black pepper to taste. Serves 2.

Submitted by: Tony Garcia, Owner & Executive Chef

Cooks Kettle Restaurant

At Victory Trade School
200 W. Commercial
Springfield, MO 65803
417-864-2210

www.victorytradeschool.org

BBQ has become one of my hobbies. I have had the opportunity to help form a professional BBQ competition team. One of my good friends Chef Steve Gibson is a big guy with a huge heart. He has owned his own BBQ restaurant in the past and has been around the professional level KCBS BBQ circuit for years. He, his wife, and I compete in several events a year using it as an educational opportunity for the trade school students. The two recipes here are two that we used in the 2005 season in the Rockin – Ribs contest in Springfield Missouri. We have been blessed with success at this event every time we go.

Little Joes BBQ Sauce

1/2 c. red wine vinegar
1-1/2 c. brown sugar
1 tsp. black pepper
2 tsp. paprika
4 Tbsp. Worcestershire
1 Tbsp. onion powder
1 tsp. chili powder
1 Tbsp. garlic powder

1/2 c. water
2 c. ketchup
2 tsp. salt
2-1/2 Tbsp. dry mustard
2 dash hot sauce
1/2 tsp. ground cayenne pepper
1/4 c. molasses

Put the following ingredients in a blender and thoroughly mix. Refrigerate what you don't use.

BBQ Rub

2 c. brown sugar
1/2 c. chili powder
1/4 c. thyme
1/4 c. garlic powder
1 c. paprika

1 c. seasoned salt
1/2 c. cumin
1/4 c. basil
1/4 c. onion powder
1 Tbsp. cayenne

Combine all ingredients.

Submitted by: Chadwick M Isom, Executive Chef

Cooks Kettle Restaurant

At Victory Trade School
200 W. Commercial
Springfield, MO 65803
417-864-2210

www.victorytradeschool.org

The Italian meatballs and homemade marinara was a set of recipes that I developed for an appearance on KLOR 10 morning show in the fall of 2006. It was a series on back-to-school meals with the whole family. It is interesting that I learned my Italian style cooking skills from a Chef Giovanni 15 years ago. He put me through culinary school and saw something in me and taught more than just cooking; he teaches principals and values. Every day he would prepare a meal before dinner service, and the entire staff would sit down together to eat. We would share about our lives and encourage each other. Chef Giovanni showed me how a family should interact. There are blessings all around me every day if I choose to see them.

Italian Meatballs

4 lbs. hamburger
1-1/2 Tbsp. garlic powder
2 Tbsp. parsley
1 tsp. black pepper
1/2 c. bread crumbs
1/2 c. onion, finely diced

1-1/2 Tbsp. Italian seasonings
1 Tbsp. sage
1 Tbsp. salt
2 eggs
2 Tbsp. Worcestershire

Mix all ingredients until combined. Make 2 inch balls. Bake at 400° for 20 minutes.

Italian Marinara

1 large onion, diced
2 ribs of celery, diced
1 - 28 oz. can tomatoes, diced
2 Tbsp. tomato paste
1 Tbsp. basil leaves
1/4 tsp. chili flake
1 tsp. sage
8 cloves garlic

2 medium carrots, diced
1/4 c. olive oil
1 - 28 oz. can tomatoes, crushed
3 bay leaves
1 tsp. oregano
1/4 tsp. mace
2 Tbsp. sugar
1 tsp. salt

Cook onion in the olive oil until soft. Add carrot and celery. Cook until soft. Add tomato paste and garlic cloves. Sauté a few minutes. Add both cans of tomato product and simmer for 20 minutes. Add all the seasonings and let set off the heat for 15 minutes. Puree in a blender or food processor. (Remove bay leaves first.)

Submitted by: Chadwick M Isom, Executive Chef

Mostaccioli

Sauce:

1-1/2 c. onions, chopped
1/3 c. olive oil
4 - 6 oz. cans tomato paste
2 Tbsp. sugar
1 tsp. pepper
7 bay leaves (remove after 30 min.)

2 cloves garlic, minced
2-1/2 cans tomato juice (qt. size)
2 c. water
1 Tbsp. salt
1 Tbsp. crushed oregano

In a big pot mix all ingredients and cook for 1 hour on simmer, stirring occasionally.

Prepare mostaccioli noodles. Cook and drain according to package directions. Mix noodles with sauce and serve with fresh grated parmesan cheese. Hamburger meat can also be added.

Submitted by: LaVerne Cantrell, Co-owner

Downtown Springfield Association

304 W McDaniel St
Springfield, MO 65806
417-831-6200

www.itsalldowntown.com

Aunt Janice's Pasta with Vodka Sauce

My Aunt Janice was one of those eccentric free spirited women that every girl should have in her life. I didn't get to see her much since she lived in Brooklyn and I lived in Springfield so anytime to see her was wonderfully special. I would always ask her about family recipes that I could keep and share with the family. The Vodka in this dish adds a unique and surprising flavor.

1/3 c. vodka
1 c. crushed tomato
1 c. heavy cream

4 Tbsp. butter
1/2 c. freshly grated parmesan
1/4 tsp. crushed red pepper, optional

In a medium saucepan melt the butter then add the vodka. Add tomatoes and cheese, bring to a boil. Add cream and pepper; serve immediately over favorite pasta.

Submitted by: Kathryn Vicat-Dlabach, UDA Community Development & Festival Assistant

Easy's Cajun Restaurant & Bar

1710 S Glenstone Ave
Springfield, MO 65804
417-881-3939

www.easysrestaurant.com

If you could turn the colorful trademarks of Mardi Gras into an edible dish, then you might find yourself at Easy's Cajun Restaurant & Bar with its soothing colors, relaxing tables and creative menu items. This family-owned and operated eatery serves each freshly prepared meal with lots of passion. Nothing but the finest ingredients go into the Southern recipes, and although they may be Asian, their hearty comfort food is very much known to be as good or better than some of the restaurants down South. With plenty of entrees and original fusion items, each dish is served hot and fresh with a side of soul.

Seafood Gumbo

2-1/2 c. medium dark roux
3 c. celery, chopped
1/2 c. tomato paste
5 lbs. Andoulle sausage, thinly sliced
1 Tbsp. sweet basil
4 whole bay leaves
1 Tbsp. kitchen bouquet
1-1/4 gal. fresh seafood stock
6 medium gumbo crabs (cleaned and split in half)
1 qt. oysters

3 c. onions, diced 1/4 inch pieces
3 c. bell peppers, diced 1/4 inch pieces
1/2 c. fresh minced garlic
1 tsp. whole thyme leaves
1 Tbsp. black pepper
1 tsp. ground cayenne pepper
2 c. crushed tomato fillets
1-1/2 lbs. catfish fillets (shanks, no bellies or bones)
1 Tbsp. gumbo file
3 lbs. fresh shrimp (peeled and deveined 31-35 count)

Use a braiser or 20 quart stock pot and over high heat, whisk the roux 3-5 minutes. Add the onions, celery, bell pepper, tomato paste and garlic to the roux and simmer over medium low heat until all vegetables are very soft. About 30 minutes. Meanwhile, sauté sausage in light oil. Discard grease, than add sausage and any gratin to the gumbo. Add remaining ingredients (except gumbo filé, oysters and shrimp) to the gumbo; simmer over low heat for 45 minutes. Break up pieces of catfish (in the gumbo) with a chef's spoon. Allow gumbo to cool for 30 minutes, cover and place overnight in the refrigerator. When ready to serve, bring gumbo to low boil; remove 2 chef spoons of stock and mix with the gumbo filé. Make a paste and add to the gumbo, whisk in completely. Add oysters and shrimp, curl the oysters and turn shrimp pink (3-5 minutes) and serve over chicken stock rice. Serve with additional gumbo filé and hot sauce if needed.

Submitted by: Kevin Kwok, Executive Chef & Owner

Hickok's Steakhouse & Brewery

314 S. Patton
Springfield, MO 65806
417-832-1141

www.hickokssteakhouse.com

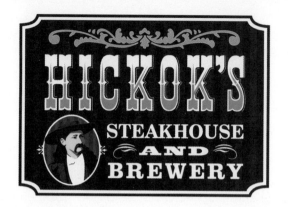

Hickok's is family friendly, fun, and affordable. "The Best Steakhouse and Brewery in Town!" Come visit the Old West in one of the oldest buildings in downtown Springfield, only a block from where the famous gunfight between Wild Bill Hickok and Dave Tutt happened in 1865. The first fast draw gunfight in America. Great Food, Great Beer, Great Fun. Lunch or Dinner, Monday through Saturday. All at a Great Price.

Seafood Steak Topper

1 Tbsp. minced garlic
2 c. seafood stock
4 oz. Gruye're cheese
2 tsp. onion powder
8 oz. shrimp
3/4 c. asparagus tips (optional)

2 c. white wine
8 oz. cream cheese
6 oz. heavy cream
1 tsp. paprika
8 oz. crab meat

Sauté garlic lightly in olive oil, then pour in wine and stock and reduce by 2/3. Lower heat to a slight simmer and add cheese, cream, and seasoning. Once melted and smooth, add seafood and asparagus. Allow time for shrimp to cook through. You can adjust thickness to your liking by adding more liquid (stock or cream). Pour over your favorite grilled meat and enjoy. We like it on sliced Tri-tip steak.

Submitted by: Jared Comer, Manager and John Burke, Chef

Honey Heaven & the Vineyard Tea Room

2516 S Campbell
Springfield, MO 65807
417-869-0233

www.honeyheaven.com

What's the Buzz...

Honey Heaven is happy to announce the opening of our Vineyard Tea Room Monday~Saturday 11am~2pm. Enjoy Healthy Gourmet Dining Bee-cause OUR FOOD IS TO LIVE FOR! The Vineyard Tea Room's Bee-licious Recipes are made from our Wonderful Raw Honey. Let's Bee Havin' a Party!

   Looking for a Place to have a Party? Well, look no further! Honey Heaven and the Vineyard Tea Room is the perfect place to have Princess Tea Parties, Women's Luncheons, Showers, Red Hatters, or any other occasions. God Bless and Thank You For Your "Bees" ness!

Honey Mustard Dip

1 c. Honey Heaven's Golden, Glorious & Pure Honey Mustard
2/3 c. mayonnaise   1/3 c. sour cream

Mix together and bee-gin dipping your favorite vegetables.

Honey Sweet Potato Casserole

2 large sweet potatoes, baked   4 Tbsp. butter
1/2 c. Honey Heaven's Golden, Glorious & Pure Honey   1/2 c. pecans

Peel baked sweet potatoes. Place into casserole dish. Add butter and pecans. Microwave for 1-2 minutes. Immediately add honey, mix well and serve.

Submitted by: Lena Meyer, "The Honey Lady"

Metro Builders Supply

3252 N Glenstone
Springfield MO 65803
417-833-1113

www.metrobuilderssupply.com

MBS

METRO BUILDERS SUPPLY
"Your Home Appliance Specialist"

Metro Builders Supply is the largest Authorized Appliance Distributor in the Midwest. With eight stores in four states, Metro has the buying power to offer the lowest possible price on more than 30 brands of major appliances. Whether you are a builder, contractor, or homeowner, Metro has the product to meet your needs and your budget. Each of our locations provides an extensive display of products, many showcased in kitchen cabinetry. Our employee-owned company prides itself with expert salespeople who offer years of appliance sales experience and extraordinary customer service. Our showroom in Springfield, MO offers an extensive lighting department as well. The largest selection, the lowest prices… experience Metro!

Angel Hair Shrimp Bake

A favorite for large groups. Featured in the Metro Experience Cookbook.

1 - 9 oz. pkg. refrigerated angel hair pasta
3/4 c. feta cheese, crumbled
1 - 16 oz. jar chunky salsa
3/4 c. fresh parsley, minced
1 tsp. dried oregano
1 c. half and half

1 1/2 lb. uncooked medium shrimp, peeled and deveined
1/2 c. Swiss cheese, shredded
1/2 c. Monterey Jack cheese, shredded
1 tsp. dried basil
2 eggs
1 c. plain yogurt

In a greased 13 x 9 inch baking dish, layer half of the pasta, shrimp, feta cheese, Swiss cheese and salsa. Repeat layers. Sprinkle with Monterey Jack cheese, parsley, basil and oregano. In a small bowl, whisk eggs, cream and yogurt; pour over casserole. Bake, uncovered at 350° for 25-30 minutes or until shrimp turn pink and pasta is tender. Let stand 5 minutes before serving. Yield: 12 Servings.

Submitted By: Judy Bilyeu, Metro Builders Supply

Metropolitan Grill

2931 East Battlefield
Springfield, MO 65804
417-889-4951

www.metropolitan-grill.com

Metropolitan Grill is the "Cheers" of fine dining. Where Spain meets Italy in the heart of the Ozarks. I love people, and I love to cook, so the restaurant is my vehicle to achieve what I love. Relax and let the atmosphere and a great glass of wine fill your senses while we create unique dishes for you in our display kitchen.

My Cooking Philosophy: 'Creation.' As an Executive Chef I challenge my kitchen staff every day to 'create, not copy'. Many artists can paint Picasso; many pianists can play Mozart; and yes, many Chefs can make Emeril's dishes. My menu is inspired by my restaurant family and my emotions. Enjoy our "creations."

Steven Pasta

Home-made chicken stock
3 c. water
2 oz. fresh basil, finely chopped
2 slices cooked bacon, chopped
1/4 c. grape tomatoes, halved
1/3 c. fresh baby spinach

1/4 c. white wine
Cornstarch
1/4 c. olive oil
1 Tbsp. black olives
1/4 c. artichoke hearts
Sliced mozzarella

Home-made Chicken Stock:
Bring 1 cup of chicken broth (brand of your choice) and 1/4 cup of white wine to a boil. Mix 3 cups of cold tap water and 1/2 cup cornstarch; whisk together. Add more corn starch, if necessary, until you have a slightly thick paste.

Steven:
Add 3 ounces chicken stock, basil, olive oil, bacon, black olives, artichoke hearts and tomatoes in an 8 inch sauté pan. Sauté all ingredients together, tossing frequently. When tomatoes begin to soften, add spinach and mozzarella. Sauté together until spinach begins to soften. Add cooked pasta of your choice.

Submitted by: Pat Duran, Owner & Executive Chef

Pappy's Place

943 N. Main Avenue
Springfield, MO 65802
417-866-8744

Pappy's Place has stood at this location since 1904. While now housing a bar/restaurant, the store first began as a family-owned shoe repair shop. Shortly after that, the owners opened a grocery store and kept it that way until the 1920s.

New owners opened a cafe on the property in 1924. Following Prohibition, the cafe applied for a beer-by-the-drink license. This license, which is still held by Pappy's, is the oldest continuous license in Springfield.

Pappy's Place may be old, and not very well-known, but it is a place of character. The people are friendly, the food is good and the beer is cold. A casual atmosphere makes for a laid-back time. For many people, it is a place of good memories.

Frog Legs with Other Stuff

8 pair frog legs
1 onion, chopped
1 Tbsp. chopped garlic
1/2 chopped (or sliced) red bell pepper
1/2 c. bourbon whiskey
1 c. white wine

1 stick butter
8 oz. baby Portobello's, sliced
Sprinkle of hot pepper flakes
Juice of 1 lemon
Salt and pepper
Flour

Separate frog legs, dredge in flour, and season with salt and pepper. Sauté slowly in butter until they brown. Add mushrooms, garlic, onion, peppers and pepper flakes. Cook for another 3 minutes. Add liquids. Simmer for another 5 minutes. Serve with rice and/or grilled garlic toast.

Jack's Deviled Eggs – From "Hades"

Wednesday night at Pappy's is traditionally "Egg Night," meaning that a friend of ours has a small farm and raises chickens to sell the eggs. The cafe is full of women, all of them talking at once. I started cooking the hard boiled eggs, and then decided to add a little heat. It didn't work…They kept on talking!

12 eggs, hard boiled, cut in half
12 pickled jalapeno slices, diced
1/2 c. mayonnaise
1/4 c. grated horseradish
Cracked black pepper

6 slices bacon, cooked crisp
1/2 onion, finely diced
1/4 c. Dijon mustard
Tabasco sauce or cayenne sauce
Salt

Remove the yolks from hard boiled eggs. Mix in the mayo, mustard, and horseradish along with a few squirts of pepper sauce. Season with salt. Chop bacon into little bits. Mix with jalapenos and onions. Reserve. In each egg white's cavity, put a drop of pepper sauce. Spoon egg yolk mixture into egg whites. Top with bacon, jalapeno, and onions. Sprinkle cracked black pepper across eggs, including exposed egg white tops.

Submitted by: Jack Rauhoff, Chef

◇◇◇◇◇◇◇◇◇◇◇◇◇◇◇◇◇◇◇◇◇◇◇◇◇◇◇◇◇◇◇◇◇◇◇◇

Peabody's

312 E. Commercial St
Springfield, Mo. 65803
417-832-8585

COME FOR THE FOOD, STAY FOR THE FUN

The idea behind Peabody's Restaurant grew from the countless family and friends we have entertained in our home. Many have enjoyed Ron's cooking and encouraged him to begin his own restaurant. We hope you get pleasure from the unique charm Peabody's provides while enjoying some of our favorite dishes. These dishes are inspired from Ron's travels throughout the world during his twenty-year career in the United States Navy. Our family has loved them, and we know you will too!

Garlic and Ranch Whipped Potatoes with Parmesan Cheese

2 lbs. red potatoes (cubed and boiled until soft)
1-1/2 tsp. garlic powder
Salt and pepper to taste.

1 c. ranch dressing
2 heaping Tbsp. butter (yummy).

While hand whipping potatoes, add the rest of the ingredients. Garnish with shredded parmesan cheese and parsley.

Submitted by: Ron Peabody, Owner

Riad Mediterranean Cuisine

105 Park Central Square
Springfield, MO 65806
417-866-1151

1250 E. Republic
Springfield, MO 65806
417-881-RIAD (7423)

www.riadcuisine.com

Since opening in February of 2004, Riad cuisine has proudly given the Springfield area a taste of the Mediterranean. With the health conscious menu, customers can enjoy a tasty meal without guilt. Meeting rooms are available at both locations. Our private rooms are conveniently located and tastefully decorated with various seating arrangements that can accommodate your needs. Ideal for meetings, parties, receptions, conferences, or retreats. Optional services include complete meals, catering, high speed internet, projection screen, TV with cable and bar service. Call to reserve.

Riad Signature Chicken Pasta

1 lb. chicken breast
3 Tbsp. lemon pepper
2 c. tomatoes, diced
2 c. feta cheese

1-1/2 lb. penne noodles
4 Tbsp. olive oil
1/2 c. parsley, chopped
2 c. mixed olive, sliced

Cut chicken breast into small cubes removing fat. Boil 1-1/2 gallons of water in a large pot. Once water is at rapid boil, pour pasta in and cook for 12-15 minutes or until tender. While pasta is cooking, heat 2 tablespoons of olive oil in a large skillet on medium high. Once skillet is hot, add chicken cubes and 1 tablespoons of lemon pepper to season chicken. Sauté chicken until crispy on edges. Cook for about 7-10 minutes or until cooked throughout. Once pasta is cooked, drain water and put into a large mixing bowl. Add 2 tablespoons of lemon pepper, 2 tablespoons of olive oil and remaining ingredients and mix well. Divide pasta into 4 separate serving bowls and top with cooked chicken. Sprinkle parsley for garnish. Serves 4.

Submitted by: Riad Matar, Owner

Springfield Brewing Company

305 South Market St
Springfield, MO 65806
417-832-TAPS (8277)

www.springfieldbrewingco.com

Springfield Brewing Company was established in 1997. As the most unique dining experience in Springfield, we feature an expansive menu, award winning hand-crafted ales and lagers, banquet facilities, outdoor dining, pool tables and live music Wednesday through Sunday. We invite you down to help us celebrate our 10 year anniversary and the opening of the College Station car park.

Santa Fe Pasta

4 c. water
2 tsp. garlic, minced
1/3 c. flour
2 oz. chipotle peppers, drained with no juice, chopped
Dash of kosher salt

2 Tbsp. chicken base
1/3 c. margarine, melted
2 red peppers, roasted, skinned and deseeded and chopped
1 c. heavy cream
1/2 tsp. white pepper   1 large bag of cooked penne pasta

In a double boiler, bring water, chicken base and minced garlic to a low boil. In a small saucepan over low heat, whisk the flour into the melted margarine and cook for about a minute. While whisking briskly, add in the flour and margarine mixture to the boiling liquid. Reduce the heat and simmer until thickened. Add roasted red peppers and chipotle peppers. Simmer for 10 minutes. Add heavy cream, salt and white pepper. Add cooked pasta and serve.

Submitted by: Kevin Mackey, Owner

15) It's All Downtown Trivia

The Heer's Tower was known for many years as:

a. "The Tallest Point Between Denver and the Alleghenies"

b. "Crown of the Queen City"   c. "Beacon of the Ozarks"

d. "Pinnacle of Park Central"

Answer on page 200

Trolley's Downtown Bar & Grille

107 Park Central Square
Springfield, MO 65806
417-799-0309

www.trolleysgrill.com

The three-story building that houses Trolley's Downtown Bar & Grille was purchased for the purpose of renovating the top two floors into luxury loft apartments. With that project completed, the first floor remained vacant for the next two years. After much thought over a vacant first floor, we came up with the idea of putting a restaurant in the space. Then we developed a concept for a restaurant that would fit into the extensive renovation of Downtown Springfield. Through our understanding of architecture and the public's fascination with the historical downtown buildings, a 1920's theme was conceived. The name Trolley's came from the mode of transportation that defined that era.

Baked Asparagus wrapped in Prosciutto

15 asparagus stalks
1 tsp. sea salt
1 tsp. black pepper

1/4 lb. prosciutto
3 oz. olive oil

Wash asparagus in cold water. Cut off 1 inch of the base of the stalk. Place in pan and toss with olive oil, salt and pepper. Let marinate for 1 hour. Wrap 3-4 inches of asparagus in thinly sliced prosciutto. Bake at 350° for 12-15 minutes or until crisp, not burnt. Oven cooking times may vary.

Pinot Noir Glazed Garlic Red Potatoes

1 tsp. olive oil
1 tsp. garlic in water
1/4 tsp. black pepper
1/4 tsp. sea salt

8 red potatoes
1/2 c. onion, chopped
1/4 tsp. garlic salt
1/2 c. Pinot Noir

Heat skillet to medium high heat. Add olive oil. When hot, add all ingredients except the wine. Cook until al dente. Add wine and cover for 8-10 minutes. Remove from heat and serve.

Submitted by: Ryan MacDonald, "The General"

Taste of Springfield

Desserts

1955 MAPLE CAFE

HOME OF THE $2.99 BREAKFAST SPECIAL – 2 EGGS, BACON, TOAST AND COFFEE

The 1955 Maple Cafe was established in 1955 just as the namesake indicates. It was built along historic Route 66 and is part of Springfield history. The new owners took over in 2007 and pride themselves on running a Christian-based establishment, with cookin' just the way mom made it. They have daily specials and a great hometown atmosphere. The customers are called family; well because they pretty much live there!

Maple-licious Coconut Cream Pie

3 c. sugar
4 egg yolks
1 tsp. vanilla
1 c. flaked coconut

1/2 c. flour
3 c. milk
1/2 tsp. butter

In a medium saucepan, combine milk, egg yolks, butter, sugar, and flour. Bring to a boil over low heat, stirring constantly. Remove from heat, and stir in 3/4 cup of the coconut and the vanilla extract. Pour into pie shell and chill 2 to 4 hours, or until firm. Top with whipped topping, and remaining 1/4 cup of coconut.

Note:
To toast coconut, spread it in an ungreased pan and bake in a 350° (175° C.) oven for 5-7 minutes, or until golden brown, stirring occasionally.

For meringue topping:
4 egg whites
1/4 c. sugar

1/4 tsp. cream of tartar

Beat egg whites and cream of tartar to a soft peak. Add sugar; beat to a stiff peak when the beater is raised. Bake at 400° until brown.

Southern Banana Pudding

2 pkgs. Jell-O instant banana pudding
1 - 8 oz. carton sour cream
1 box Nabisco vanilla wafers

3 c. milk
1 large Cool Whip
5 medium sized bananas

Mix the pudding with milk by hand. Add sour cream and cool whip to the pudding mixture. In your serving dish make layers of vanilla wafers, bananas and pudding mixture. Let it set for several hours or overnight to allow your wafers to soften. (For a lighter version, substitute sugar free, fat free and low fat items to the recipe.)

Submitted by: Larry & Hollie Davis, Owners

Andy's Frozen Custard

Springfield
2119 N. Glenstone
3147 E. Sunshine
2726 S. Campbell Ave.
4420 S. Campbell Ave.

Branson
3415 W. Hwy 76

888-60-ANDYS

www.eatandys.com

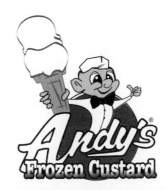

Andy's has made a science out of frozen custard. We've perfected the method for preparing and serving custard in its highest form, giving you an unparalleled frozen treat. We use the finest ingredients in our mix, a secret recipe of milk, cream, sugar and eggs, which is processed and shipped to Andy's stores within 24 hours to maintain ultimate freshness. Our proprietary frozen custard machines (less than ten are manufactured each year) are customized to Andy's exacting specifications. Andy's Frozen Custard is made fresh hourly and only served at its peak flavor potential of sixty minutes to ensure that our customers get the best frozen custard each time they visit. It's just part of the Andy's difference.

Angel Cookies

Carol Kuntz brought this recipe from Montana after visiting Mervy & Eileen Long.

1 c. shortening
1/2 c. brown sugar
1 tsp. vanilla
1 tsp. soda
1/2 tsp. salt

1/2 c. white sugar
1 egg
2 c. flour
1 tsp. cream of tartar
1/2 c. chopped nuts

Cream shortening and sugars; add egg and vanilla. Beat, then add sifted dry ingredients and nuts. Roll dough in small balls; dip top half in cold water, then in sugar and flatten slightly on greased cookie sheet. (Colored sugar makes pretty holiday cookies.) Bake at 350° for 12 min.

Raisin Cream Pie

3/4 c. raisins
1/4 c. cornstarch
3 c. milk
3 Tbsp. butter or margarine
1 - 9 oz. baked pie shell

1 c. sugar
1/4 tsp. salt
4 eggs, separated
1-1/2 tsp. vanilla

Boil raisins until soft; drain and set aside. Combine sugar, cornstarch and salt and gradually stir in milk. Cook and stir over medium heat until bubbly. Separate eggs and beat yolks slightly. Stir one cup of hot mixture into egg yolks, then return egg mixture to saucepan and bring to boil. Remove from heat, stir in butter, vanilla and raisins. Pour into baked shell. Beat egg whites for meringue and spread over filling. Bake at 350° for 12-15 min.

Submitted by: Carol Kuntz, Vice President, Founder and Andy's Mom

Argentina Steakhouse

1410 E. Republic road
Springfield, MO 65804
417-886-8010

www.theargentinasteakhouse.com

The Argentina Steakhouse was established in March 2002 in Springfield, Missouri. The family and original staff from Buenos Aries, Argentina opened this independent restaurant in hopes of introducing the people of Springfield to a true steakhouse in the tradition of great cities. As "Springfield's Premiere Steakhouse," the Argentina Steakhouse strives to offer the highest quality and best service to our patrons.

Argentina Style Vanilla Flan

2 tsp. vanilla
1/2 c. sugar
1 can condensed milk
1 c. milk

2-1/2 Tbsp. water
4 eggs, separated
1 can evaporated milk

In a saucepan, combine sugar and water. Boil until a dark orange color. Then empty mixture into the bottom of a pan and coat sides. Let cool. In a bowl, stir egg yolks and add all milks. Then add vanilla. Stir mixture well. In a different bowl begin whipping egg whites until fluffy. Fold egg whites into mixture. Lastly, pour mixture into caramelized sugar-coated pan. Place pan in larger roasting or baking pan. Begin adding hot water until it reaches halfway up the sides of the caramelized sugar-coated pan. Bake flan in water one hour or until set in center. Let cool, then cover and chill overnight. Allow flan to come to room temperature. Run a sharp knife around the edge to loosen. Place a serving plate that's slightly larger than the pie pan on top of the pie pan, and flip upside down. Gently remove the pie pan and cut the flan into wedges to serve.

Submitted by: Angel Kim, Executive Chef

Beth's Bake Shoppe
& Tea Room

1645-D W. Republic Rd
Springfield, MO 65807
417-866-5533

www.bethsbakeshoppe.com

Beth's Bake Shoppe
and Tea Room

Beth's Bake Shoppe & Tea Room serves lunch Monday - Saturday made with delicious homemade recipes and ingredients. Our soups, quiche and specialty desserts change daily. Our fresh chicken salad has our special touch served on toasted raisin bread. Quiche has unique combinations to tempt your taste buds. Come in and check out our bakery case full of homemade cookies, bars, pies and cheesecakes. Specialty birthday, wedding and all-occasion cakes done by order only. You ruff and tuff guys don't let the tea room name scare you off. All are welcome, so come in and enjoy.

Pineapple Do Nothing Cake

Most of the recipes that we serve at Beth's Bake Shoppe & Tea Room are recipes that have been handed down from generation to generation. This pineapple do nothing cake is a popular dessert that came from my Grandma Brewer. This cake is easy to make, and your family and friends will love it. It's great on a hot summer day with homemade ice cream or on a cold winter day just out of the oven.

2 c. flour
2 whole eggs
1 tsp. baking soda
20 oz. can crushed pineapple (not drowned)

2 c. granulated sugar
1 tsp. vanilla
1/2 tsp. salt

Preheat oven to 350°. Blend flour, sugar and baking soda together. Add vanilla, eggs, salt, and crushed pineapple; stir together just until well mixed. Pour into a greased cookie sheet. Bake 20-25 minutes.

Icing:
1/2 c. butter
2/3 c. evaporated milk
1 tsp. vanilla
1 c. coconut

1 c. granulated sugar
1 tsp. salt
1 c. pecans

Make icing while cake is baking. Place ingredients in small sauce pan and simmer over low heat. Pour over hot cake when it comes out of the oven. Serve hot or cold..

Submitted by: Beth Perry, Owner

Cooks Kettle Restaurant

At Victory Trade School
200 W. Commercial
Springfield, MO 65803
417-864-2210

www.victorytradeschool.org

Named for Everett and Esther Cook, founders of Springfield Victory Mission, the Cook's Kettle Restaurant provides the culinary laboratory setting for VTS. This restaurant, newly remodeled with a "French Bistro" look, has 2 classically French trained chefs instructing the students as they attend classes in Victory Trade School and receive hands-on training while working various positions in the restaurant. The customers of Cook's Kettle Restaurant agree they return because of the high quality of the food, the low prices, and the cleanliness of the facility. This economical place to eat is a model of how a restaurant can serve good food and practice good hygiene and sanitation. This "student-operated" restaurant provides variety in the menu and all customers are served with professionalism.

Holiday Stratta

Stratta:

6 eggs	1/2 c. white sugar
1-1/2 c. milk	1/2 c. heavy cream
8 c. cubed bread (stale works best i.e.: bread, rolls, and croissants	1/2 c. dried fruit
1 tsp. pumpkin pie spice	1 tsp. salt

Topping:

1/4 c. brown sugar	1/3 c. chopped nuts

Method:

Cut bread into small bite-sized cubes, about 1/4 inch size. In a small mixing bowl, mix bread and dried fruits thoroughly. Place into a round, deep sided baking dish (I suggest minimum 10 inch diameter).

In a separate bowl, whisk the eggs, white sugar, milk, heavy cream, pumpkin pie spice and salt until fully mixed. Pour this mixture over the top of the bread. Cover with plastic wrap and press down lightly on the mixture to help the bread absorb the liquid. Rewrap the baking dish and refrigerate overnight.

To bake, preheat your oven to 350° F. Take plastic wrap off the baking dish. Mix the nuts and sugar together to form your topping. Sprinkle an even layer of the mixture over the Stratta. Place in the oven and bake 20-25 minutes, or until a toothpick comes out clean... kind of like checking a cake! Allow Stratta to cool for at least 10 minutes and serve with either a vanilla sauce or a fruit sauce. Yields 12 pie style slices.

Submitted by: Chef Bill Luten

Country Deli Cakes and Catering

1325 S Glenstone Ave
Springfield, MO 65804
417-887-9244

www.julieschewies.com

Country Deli Cakes and Catering has been Serving Springfield, MO since 1984. We Specialize In: Wedding & All Occasion Cakes, Hot & Cold Hors D'oeuvres, Full Menu Catering, Wedding Receptions, Rehearsal Dinners, Business Functions, Church Functions, Private Parties, Anniversaries and Retirements. Our wedding cakes are moist and delicious and only made using quality ingredients! We also custom design grooms cakes. Each cake is designed to meet your personal specifications.

Peanut Butter Fudge

2 c. sugar
1/4 c. cream

1/2 c. syrup
1 stick butter

Boil above ingredients for 1 minute, then pour into bowl. Add 3/4 cup creamy or crunchy peanut butter. Beat about 5 minutes, then pour into buttered dish.

Peanut Brittle

1 c. white sugar
1/2 c. water
1 tsp. vanilla
1 tsp. soda

1/2 c. white syrup (Karo)
1 c. raw peanuts
1 Tbsp. butter, softened

Generously butter a cookie sheet. Measure all the ingredients and have on hand because the process will move very fast. Heat the sugar, white syrup and water in a heavy skillet (preferably iron) and boil until it threads. When the spoon is lifted out of the mixture, light, floating threads should form like cobwebs in the wind. Add the raw peanuts and continue to boil until the peanuts are popping and turning a golden brown-be careful not to burn them. Add the vanilla, soda and butter. This will cause the peanut caramel mixture to spatter and foam. Stir until just mixed and the bubbles have not been worked out (this creates a lighter texture). Do this as you are walking to the cookie sheet and pour the mixture onto the sheet to cool. When cool, break into pieces.

Submitted by: LaVerne Cantrell, Co-owner

Fedora Social House

On The Square Downtown
300 Park Central East
Springfield, MO 65806
417-832-9514

www.fedoradowntown.com

When it's time to decompress from the day's events, you do have lots of choices in Springfield. If you're looking for urbane and polished, yet comfortable and unhurried, Fedora Social House is your easy answer to the evening. Is your office in the downtown area? Come share one of our delicious cheese fondues with friends from work. Look no further than Fedora Social House for a unique venue to host your private party or corporate function. You'll make a great impression on friends and associates with an extensive spread of desserts, fondues, and more!

Godiva Mudcake

Fedora Social House's take on the dessert party favorite.

1 oz. vanilla vodka
Scoop of ice cream
Sprig of mint

1/2 oz. Godiva chocolate liqueur
Crushed Oreos
1 gummy worm

Blend liquor and ice cream. Pour into any cocktail glass, but it looks best in a large martini glass.
Sprinkle a liberal amount of crushed Oreos on the top of the dessert, evenly covering the top. Garnish with a sprig of mint and a gummy worm. Basically, it supposed to look like a plant.

Strawberry Lemonade Shortcake

Fedora Social House's crisp summer treat.

1 slice of any lemon tart or cake
1 box strawberries

Whipped cream
1/2 c. strawberry puree or daiquiri mix

Place tart in center of plate. Create a barrier around the tart using whipped cream. Create another barrier of sliced strawberries around the whipped cream. Pour puree over the top of everything.
Garnish with a lemon, strawberry, or drizzle with white chocolate.

Submitted by: Drex Holt, Manager

First Friday Art Walk

411 N. Sherman Parkway
Springfield, Missouri 65802
417-849-8255

www.ffaw.org

First Friday Art Walk, held 6-10 p.m. the first Friday of each month, is a free walking tour of downtown Springfield's 20-plus art galleries. The event features works by local, regional and national artists, as well as live demonstrations and performances, all in support of First Friday Art Walk's nonprofit mission of promoting fine art and economic vitality in the Downtown Arts District. For more information, give us a call or visit our website.

Milk Chocolate Cheesecake with Muscato Wine & Blackberry Sauce

2 c. chocolate cookie crumbs (such as Oreos or chocolate wafers)
1/4 lb. unsalted butter, melted (1 stick
1 c. plus 2 Tbsp. sugar
1/2 c. heavy cream
Pinch of salt
4 oz. milk chocolate, melted in microwave
2 pt. fresh blackberries (or thawed if frozen)
1 Tbsp. confectioners' sugar

1-1/2 lbs. cream cheese, softened
3 large eggs
1/4 c. bleached all-purpose flour
1 tsp. pure vanilla extract
1/4 c. Muscato sweet dessert wine
1 c. heavy cream
Sprigs of fresh mint, garnish

Preheat the oven to 350° F. Combine the cookie crumbs and melted butter in a medium bowl, and mix thoroughly. With your fingers, press into the bottom and slightly up the sides of a 10-inch spring-form pan. In a food processor or in a large bowl using an electric mixer, beat the cream cheese until smooth. Add 1 cup of the sugar and process. Add the eggs 1 at a time, running the processor in between each addition. Add the heavy cream, flour, salt and vanilla, and process until smooth, scraping down the sides of the bowl as needed. With the motor running, add the chocolate in a steady stream. Pour the mixture into the prepared pan. Bake until the center of the cake sets but the center is slightly wobbly, 1 hour to 1 hour and 15 minutes.

Remove from the oven and loosen the sides of the cake with a thin knife. Let cool on a wire rack. Refrigerate until well chilled, at least 3 hours. In a medium bowl, combine the Muscato wine, blackberries, and remaining 2 tablespoons of sugar. Mash slightly with the back of a spoon to lightly crush the berries and combine. Cover and refrigerate for 2 hours.

In a clean bowl, whip the cream until soft peaks start to form. Add the confectioners' sugar and whip to stiff peaks. To serve, un-mold the cheesecake. Slice with a sharp knife dipped in hot water and place on dessert plates. Spoon the berries onto each serving and top with the whipped cream. Garnish with the mint sprigs. Yield: Makes one 10 inch cheesecake; 12 servings.

Submitted by: Sandra CH Smith, Innkeeper & Exec. Director, Springfield Regional Arts Council

Jana's Banana Pudding

5 oz. pkg. sugar-free French vanilla pudding
1 can Eagle Brand fat-free sweetened condensed milk
12 oz. carton Cool Whip Lite
2-3 pkg. Pepperidge Farm Chessmen Cookies

2 c. skim milk
8 oz. light cream cheese, well softened
4 med. bananas

Combine pudding and milk in a bowl and beat well. In separate bowl beat together softened cream cheese and Eagle Brand until smooth. Fold in Cool Whip. Fold cream cheese mixture into pudding mixture until blended. Put one package of cookies on the bottom of a 13 x 9 inch pan. Top with sliced bananas. Top with all the pudding. Cover pudding with whole Chessmen cookies. (You might want to open both bags and use the crumbly ones on the bottom layer or buy three bags to ensure you have enough whole cookies for the top and bottom).

Submitted by: Ginny Haymes, Bellwether Gallery of the Arts

16) It's All Downtown Trivia

Minor League baseball was once played at which Springfield stadium?

a. Doling Park   b. White City Park (Boonville and Division)

c. Meador Park   d. Grant Beach Park

Answer on page 200

Global Fayre

324 S Campbell
Springfield, MO 65806
417- 873-9792

www.globalfayre.com

Buying Fair Trade has always been important to us. After our youngest daughter was born, we wanted to find something that we could do together, something that we believed in and that would benefit the wider, global community. We also shared a love of artisan products from Asia, Africa and South America, and so it was a natural choice for us to launch Global Fayre, with the mission of bringing Fair Trade products to southwest Missouri.

Oat and Chocolate Cupcake

Great Cupcakes with very little fat, especially if you use skimmed milk. Adapted from "The Bitter Sweet World of Chocolate - Sumptuous recipes using fair trade chocolate" by Troth Wells and Nikki van der Gaag

1 c. flour
1/2 c. cocoa (Fair Trade of course!)
1-1/2 tsp. baking soda
1 egg
1 tsp. vanilla (did you know you can get Fair Trade vanilla now?)
1 c. brown sugar (yes yes - Fair Trade!)

1/2 c. oats
1-1/2 tsp. baking powder
1/2 tsp. salt
1 Tbsp. oil (Fair Trade olive oil is perfect for this)
1/2 tsp. cinnamon
1/4 c. milk

Heat oven to 350º F. Combine the flour with the oats, cocoa, baking powder, baking soda and salt. In a large bowl, beat together the egg, oil, vanilla, cinnamon and sugar. Stir in the flour mixture, gradually adding the milk until just combined. Pour the batter into paper cake cups. Bake for 20-25 minutes or until a skewer comes out clean. Let the cupcakes cool on a wire rack.

Submitted by: Cheri and David Crump, Owners

Hickok's Steakhouse & Brewery

314 S. Patton
Springfield, MO 65806
417-832-1141

www.hickokssteakhouse.com

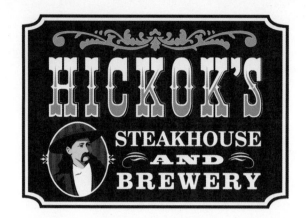

Hickok's is family friendly, fun, and affordable. "The Best Steakhouse and Brewery in Town!" Come visit the Old West in one of the oldest buildings in downtown Springfield, only a block from where the famous gunfight between Wild Bill Hickok and Dave Tutt happened in 1865. The first fast draw gunfight in America. Great Food, Great Beer, Great Fun. Lunch or Dinner, Monday through Saturday. All at a Great Price.

Cream Cake with Brandied Berries

Berries:
- 1 pint strawberries
- 1 c. sugar
- 2 oz. brandy
- 1 pint blueberries
- Juice and zest of 1 orange

Cake:
- 2 c. flour
- 2 tsp. baking powder
- 1-1/2 c. heavy cream
- 1/2 tsp. salt
- 1-1/2 c. sugar
- 2 eggs

Mix together and let set for one hour

Preheat oven to 325°. Mix all cake ingredients and pour into a greased 9 x 13 inch pan. Bake for 35 to 45 minutes or until a toothpick inserted in the middle comes out clean. Let cool for at least 30 minutes before cutting. Top cake with berry mixture and whipped cream.

Submitted by: Jared Comer, Manager and John Burke, Chef

Julie's Chewies Gourmet Sweet Shoppe

1325 S. Glenstone
Springfield, MO 65804
417-887-2777

www.julieschewies.com

Julie's **Chewies**

When it comes to cookies - we are the best. Our customers rarely leave empty handed and are always excited to see what we'll come up with next. Whether it's a birthday or a retirement party, a baby shower or just to let someone know you're thinking of them, Julie's Chewies are always a success. Our special chewy cookies also make wonderful Christmas gifts for a personal touch or for business clients. We are also known for having the largest cookie jar selection in the Springfield area along with teapots, picture frames, and many other gift ideas. Come to our shoppe to browse our large retail section specializing in gourmet foods.

Magic Cookie Bars

1/4 c. butter

1 c. graham cracker crumbs

Mix together and pat into pan to form crust.

1 c. coconut, shredded
1 can Eagle Brand milk

6 oz. pkg. chocolate and/or peanut butter chips

Layer ingredients on crust. First add shredded coconut, then chocolate and/or peanut butter chips and finally the sweetened condensed milk on top and bake at 325° for 30 minutes.

Submitted by: Betty Cantrell (Famous Cookie Bar Maker)

Molasses Cookies

3/4 c. shortening
1/4 c. molasses
2 c. unsifted flour
1/2 tsp. cinnamon
1/4 tsp. ginger

1 c. sugar
1 egg
2 tsp. soda
1/4 tsp. allspice

Cream shortening and sugar, then add molasses and egg. Stir in remaining ingredients. Roll into balls and cover with sugar. Bake at 350° on ungreased sheet for about 10-12 minutes.

Submitted by: JoAnn Harrison, Co-owner

Metro Builders Supply

3252 N Glenstone
Springfield MO 65803
417-833-1113

www.metrobuilderssupply.com

METRO BUILDERS SUPPLY
"Your Home Appliance Specialist"

Metro Builders Supply is the largest appliance distributor in the Midwest. With nine stores in four states, Metro has the buying power to offer the lowest possible price on more than 30 brands of major appliances. Whether you are a builder, contractor, or homeowner, Metro has the product to meet your needs and your budget. Each of our locations provides an extensive display of products, many showcased in kitchen cabinetry. Our employee-owned company prides itself with expert salespeople who offer years of appliance sales experience and extraordinary customer service. Our showroom in Springfield, MO offers an extensive lighting department as well. The largest selection, the lowest prices… experience Metro!

Old South Chess Pie

A delicious dessert from the Old South passed down through generations. First featured in the Metro Experience Cookbook.

1 unbaked refrigerated pie crust or frozen pie shell
3 Tbsp. flour
2 Tbsp. melted butter
1 Tbsp. fresh lemon juice

1-1/2 c. sugar
3 eggs, beaten
1-1/2 c. buttermilk

Preheat oven to 350°. If using a refrigerated pie crust, fit into a pie plate, trim and crimp edges and set aside. Combine sugar and flour in a medium bowl. Add the eggs, butter, buttermilk and lemon juice and mix well. Pour into the prepared pie shell. Bake 50 minutes to 1 hour, until pie is set. Remove from oven and cool on a rack for 30 minutes. Refrigerate several hours or overnight before serving.

White Chocolate Macadamia Nut Cookies

Delicious cookies first featured in the Metro Experience Cookbook.

1/2 c. shortening
1-1/4 c. brown sugar, firmly packed
2 Tbsp. water
1-3/4 c. flour
1/4 tsp. salt
1 c. macadamia nuts, coarsely chopped

1/4 c. butter
1 egg
1 Tbsp. vanilla
3/4 tsp. baking soda
1 c. white chocolate chips

Preheat oven to 375°. In a large mixing bowl cream shortening, butter and sugar together. Beat in egg, water and vanilla. In small bowl combine flour, baking soda and salt. Add to creamed mixture, stirring until just combined. Fold in chips and nuts. Drop by rounded teaspoon onto ungreased baking sheet. Cook 8-10 minutes.

Submitted By: Judy Bilyeu, Metro Builders Supply

The Mudhouse

323 South Ave
Springfield, MO 65806
417-832-1720

www.mudhousecoffee.com

Your Downtown Coffeehouse

When it comes to the way Mudhouse Coffee does business, one word says it all. "Freshness." With coffee, and enjoying a delicious cup of coffee, freshness is the only thing that really matters. What we can guarantee to our customers is that Mudhouse Coffee will be the freshest coffee available. We micro roast our coffee in small batches when we need it, so you never have to worry about our coffee sitting and losing the crucial freshness that is so important. It doesn't matter whether you purchase our coffee inside the coffeehouse or from the website; we guarantee it will be the freshest, best tasting coffee available! Open Monday-Friday 7:00am - Midnight, Saturday 7:00am - Midnight and Sunday 8:30am - 11:00pm.

Mudhouse Vegan Cookies

Former Mudhouse baker (and forever a part of the Mudhouse family) Mandi Hubbs, who recently moved to Portland, Oregon to pursue other interests, wanted to add a delicious all vegan recipe to our treat selection. The result has become a yummy cookie loved by all.

3 c. vegan margarine*
3 c. brown sugar
2 c. soy milk
2 tsp. baking soda
1 tsp. ground cloves
1 tsp. nutmeg
4 c. dried cranberries

1-1/3 c. sugar
4 tsp. vanilla
4 c. flour
1 tsp. powdered ginger
2 heaping tsp. cinnamon
12 c. oats
2 c. walnuts, chopped

*It is important to make sure the margarine does not have lactose or whey in the ingredients. Usually, Mudhouse bakers use Smart Balance.

Cream together the margarine and sugars until smooth. Add vanilla and soy milk and mix well. Add flour, baking soda and spices until well mixed, then stir in oats, cranberries and walnuts. Spoon out 4 ounces of batter and spread flat on a baking sheet. Bake at 325° until slightly brown but still soft. Makes at least a dozen cookies!

Submitted by: Rob Weislocher, Co-owner

Mutual of Omaha

Brian Askins Division Office
1435 E Bradford Pkwy, Suite 105
Springfield, MO 65804
417-863-7250

brian.askins@mutualofomaha.com

What are your dreams? At Mutual of Omaha-Springfield, our professional representatives can help you create a plan to reach your financial dreams with a complete line of insurance and financial products including; Life Insurance, Disability Income insurance, Annuities, Medicare Supplement insurance, and Long-Term Care insurance. Just like you, we care about our community, we support the Urban Districts Alliance-Taste of Springfield Cookbook and the dreams they want to reach for our community. Contact us today to start planning how to reach your dreams.

Chocolate-Hazelnut Ravioli

16 wonton wrappers
1 c. Nutella chocolate-hazelnut spread
16 fresh mint leaves
Granulated sugar, for dredging

1 egg, beaten to blend
Vegetable oil, for frying
Nonstick vegetable oil spray
Powdered sugar, for dusting

Line a baking sheet with plastic wrap. Place 1 wonton wrapper on the work surface. Brush the edges of the wrapper lightly with egg. Spoon 1 tablespoon of chocolate-hazelnut spread into the center of the wrapper. Fold the wrapper diagonally in half over the filling and press the edges of the wrapper to seal. Place the ravioli on the prepared baking sheet. Repeat with the remaining wonton wrappers, egg, and chocolate-hazelnut spread.

Preheat the oven to 200° F. Add enough oil to a heavy large frying pan to reach a depth of 2 inches. Heat the oil over medium heat to 350° F. Working in batches, carefully add the ravioli to the hot oil and cook until they are golden brown, about 45 seconds per side. Using a slotted spoon, transfer the ravioli to a plate lined with paper towels to drain. Then, transfer the cooked ravioli to another baking sheet and keep them warm in the oven while frying the remaining ravioli.

Note:
The fried ravioli can be prepared 1 day ahead. Cool them completely, then cover and refrigerate. Before serving, place them on a baking sheet and re-warm in a preheated 375° F oven just until they are heated through, about 7 minutes.

Spray the top side of the mint leaves very lightly with nonstick spray. Working with 1 leaf at a time, dredge the coated side of the leaves in sugar to coat lightly. Arrange 2 fried ravioli on each plate. Dust the ravioli with powdered sugar. Garnish with the sugared mint leaves and serve.

Submitted by: Lori Cloninger, Brian Askins Mutual of Omaha Division Office

Nonna's Italian American Café

306 South Ave
Springfield, MO 65806
417-831-1222

www.nonnascafe.com

Funky, Fun, Eclectic, and Relaxed, Nonna's Italian American Café has been a downtown classic for over 12 years. Delicious Food, Homemade Desserts, Friendly Prices and a Full Bar. Featuring Full-Service Catering, Event Planning, A Jazz Guitarist Duo on Thursday Night, A Classical Guitarist on Friday Night, A Jazz Guitarist on Saturday Night, A Musical Theatre Open-Mic Sunday Night called 'The Cast Party,' Monthly Operazzi Nights, and Monthly Art Shows. Join us for the First Friday Art Walk. Open Daily. Locally World Famous.

Almond Joy Cake

1 two-layer Devil's Food Cake (recipe follows)
1 c. milk
1-3/4 c. flaked sweetened coconut
2 c. toasted almonds, chopped

3/4 c. sugar
24 large marshmallows
1 recipe Chocolate Frosting (recipe follows)

As the cakes are cooling, mix sugar, milk and marshmallows in a saucepan. Cook until marshmallows melt, then add coconut. Cake layers should be cool enough to handle with your bare hands before the marshmallow mixture is applied. Spread 1/2 of the mixture on the bottom layer of the cake, add the top layer and spread the rest of the mixture over the top. Frost with chocolate frosting. Lightly press chopped toasted almonds around the outside of the cake to finish. Makes one 9 inch round cake

Devil's Food Cake with Chocolate Frosting

2 c. sugar
2 eggs
2 tsp. baking soda
2-1/4 c. flour
2 tsp. vanilla extract

1 c. vegetable or canola oil
1 c. buttermilk
1/4 tsp. salt
2/3 c. cocoa powder (such as Hershey's)
1 c. boiling water

Preheat oven to 350° F. Grease and flour two 9 inch round cake pans, and line with parchment paper cut to fit the bottom of the cake pans. Using whisk attachment on your mixer or electric beaters, mix all ingredients except the boiling water for 30 seconds. Add boiling water and mix on low speed for 30 seconds. Scrape the bowl and increase speed to medium until batter is fluffy, about 2 minutes. Pour into prepared cake pans and bake for 35-40 minutes, or until a toothpick inserted into the center of the cakes comes out clean.

Chocolate Frosting:

1 c. butter, softened but still cool	3/4 c. cocoa powder (such as Hershey's)
1/4 tsp. salt	4 c. powdered sugar, sifted
1/3 c. half and half	1 tsp. vanilla extract

In mixing bowl, cream butter (use paddle attachment if using a standing mixer) until light and fluffy, about 1 minute. Add cocoa powder and salt, and beat until smooth; scrape bowl. Add powdered sugar, 1/2 cup at a time. After all powdered sugar is incorporated, scrape bowl. While mixer is at medium speed, add half and half by the teaspoon until the frosting reaches a spreadable consistency.

Submitted by: Julia Anderson, Co-owner and Pastry Chef

◇◇◇◇◇◇◇◇◇◇◇◇◇◇◇◇◇◇◇◇◇◇◇◇◇◇◇◇◇◇◇◇◇◇◇◇◇◇◇

Parlor 88 Lounge

1111 E. Republic Rd
Springfield, MO 65807
417-882-8882

www.parlor88.com

Parlor 88 is the place to meet for cocktails and conversation. The decor is modern, and the atmosphere is decidedly trendy. The full-service bar offers an extensive martini menu along with other frozen concoctions. Sophisticated table appetizers and tempting dessert selections complete your experience at Parlor 88. Open Monday - Saturday 3:00 pm - 1:00 am. Patio and fireplace seating available.

Ice Cream Pie

1 turtle cheesecake	3 large scoops cookie dough ice cream
1 gram-cracker pie crust	1 shot Starbucks cream liquor
1 tsp. cinnamon	1 tsp. sugar
1 tsp. nutmeg	

Allow ice cream to melt, mix cheesecake with ice cream, and add dry ingredients. Place in pie crust. Freeze and serve.

Submitted by: Seth Elliott, General Manager

Peabody's

COME FOR THE FOOD, STAY FOR THE FUN

The idea behind Peabody's Restaurant grew from the countless family and friends we have entertained in our home. Many have enjoyed Ron's cooking and encouraged him to begin his own restaurant. We hope you get pleasure from the unique charm Peabody's provides while enjoying some of our favorite dishes. These dishes are inspired from Ron's travels throughout the world during his twenty-year career in the United States Navy. Our family has loved them, and we know you will too!

Caramel Apple Cobbler

This recipe is sooooooo easy, but sooooooo good!!!

2 - 16 oz. cans of apple pie filling
1 piecrust, un-baked
1 Tbsp. cinnamon
1 egg white

Caramel ice cream topping to taste
3 Tbsp. sugar
1 stick butter or margarine
2 tsp. water

Preheat oven to 350°. In a 9 x 13 inch pan spread pie filling. Sprinkle cinnamon and sugar mixture over filling. (I use a 3 to 1 ratio: 3 parts sugar to 1 part cinnamon.) Drop dollops of butter or margarine (we admit, we prefer butter; it makes it richer) over the pie filling. Drizzle caramel ice cream topping over the pie filling and butter (don't be sparing; the more goo the better). Cover with prepared pie crust. Cut several slits in top of crust so steam can escape. Using one egg white with a little water, make an egg wash and brush on top of crust. Sprinkle sugar over crust and bake for 30-40 minutes until golden brown.

Submitted by: Glenda Mitchell, Catering Coordinator

Recipe Publishers

2049 E. Cherry Street
Springfield, MO 65802
417-873-2267

www.recipepubs.com

Recipe Publishers is based in the beautiful Ozarks city of Springfield, Missouri. We produce, publish and help promote many kinds of cookbooks: *Family's Favorites, Fundraiser Cookbooks, Chefs' Collections, Restaurant Recipes, Sports Teams Cookbooks. plus many more*. **"If You Can Cook It - We Can Print It."** We'll help with each step in the process of creating the best cookbooks possible.

Chewy Oatmeal Cookies

3/4 c. butter, softened
1/4 c. date sugar
1 egg
1-1/2 tsp. vanilla
1/3 c. whole wheat flour
1/2 tsp. baking soda
1/2 tsp. cinnamon
1 c. walnuts, chopped

1/4 c. honey
1/2 c. brown sugar
1/3 c. milk
3 c. quick oats
2/3 c. unbleached flour
1/2 tsp. salt
1 c. raisins

Heat oven to 350°. Grease baking sheets with non-stick spray. Combine first 7 ingredients in large bowl. Beat at medium speed with electric mixer until well blended. Stir in oats, flours, baking soda, salt, and cinnamon. Add raisins and nuts. Drop rounded tablespoons of dough 2 inches apart onto baking sheet. Bake 9-11 minutes or until lightly browned. Makes 2-1/2 dozen cookies.

Submitted by: Pam Eddings, Cookbook Assistant Editor

Rendezvous Coffee Lounge

320 Park Central West
Springfield MO 65806
417-868-0110

Rendezvous Coffee Lounge is Springfield's newest coffee shop. However, we are much more than just another coffee shop; we feature a menu with breakfast, lunch and dinner items. We are the only place in town to get a fresh brewed cup of Turkish coffee. Our pastries and cookies are fresh-baked daily, including our famous No-Bake cookies. We are in the old Randy Bacon Gallery on Park Central West. Stop by the next time you come downtown.

Rendezvous No-Bake Cookies

This recipe was tweaked by my wife at my first coffee shop, Metro Mocha.
It was designed to be a great treat anyone can make.

4 c. sugar
1 c. cocoa
1 c. milk
2 sticks of butter

1 c. peanut butter
6 c. quick oats
2 tsp. vanilla

Combine sugar, milk, cocoa and butter. Bring to a full boil. Let boil for 2 minutes. Remove from heat and quickly mix in vanilla, oats and peanut butter. Mix well and drop on wax paper while mixture is still HOT.

Tip:
Use a 2 ounce ice cream scoop to form uniform, round cookies.

Submitted By: Submitted by: Sean and John Fleming, Owners

Tonic Ultralounge

317 Park Central East
Springfield, MO 65806
417-863-7575

www.tonicultralounge.com

Tonic Ultralounge serves as a chic gathering spot ideal for cocktails, conversation and award winning cuisine. Guests will be transported from the Queen City to a world of intrigue with a mixture of elegance and nightclub experience. Savor signature elixirs, designed exclusively for Tonic Ultralounge while experiencing exquisite cuisine prepared by the exceptional talents of our executive chef and his experienced culinary team.

Banana Chimichanga

1/4 c. chocolate chips
2 caramel squares, quartered
1 egg, beaten
1 fresh strawberry

1 banana
1 large flour tortilla
1 large scoop vanilla bean ice cream (see recipe)
1 small handful spicy fried walnuts (see recipe)

First peel your banana, and then put the tortilla in the microwave for 20 seconds or so until it's warm and flexible. Lay the banana across the tortilla, then put the chocolate chips and caramel chunks along the whole banana. Fold the edges over the tips of the banana and brush all the edges with the beaten egg. Fold the back section to the banana and roll. After resting for a couple minutes, deep fry at 375° until golden brown. Top with a scoop of homemade vanilla bean ice cream, sliced strawberries, fried walnuts, chocolate and caramel sauces.

Vanilla Bean Ice Cream:

10 c. heavy cream
Pinch salt
24 egg yolks
Thermometer

5 c. whole milk
3 vanilla beans (seeded)
2 c. sugar

Combine all ingredients except eggs, 1 cup sugar and all of the seeded vanilla bean then, slowly bring up to 175° F; turn off heat, cover and let set for 15 minutes. Combine: all eggs and 1 cup sugar; whisk until pale yellow. Add the hot mixture into the eggs, slowly at first so you don't have scrambled eggs! Place back on heat until it thickens about 10 minutes, then strain and refrigerate for at least 24 hours. Churn and enjoy!! For breakfast the next day, use the egg whites for a healthy omelet!!

Spicy Fried Walnuts:

6 c. raw walnuts
Cayenne pepper to taste

4 c. powdered sugar

Boil the walnuts for 30 minutes on a rapid boil with lots of water. Then mix the powdered sugar and cayenne until its looks a little pink (if you want it less spicy add a 1/3 cup) with a wire whisk. After draining the water off the walnuts dredge the wet nuts in the sugar; after coating them, deep fry at 375° for 2-3 minutes or until they all float, but be careful. Don't over fry them; they're a little tricky, but well worth it!

Submitted by: Tonic Ultralounge

Tower Club

The Hammons Tower
901 E Saint Louis St # 2100
Springfield, MO 65806
(417) 866-4466

www.towerclubspringfield.com

The Tower Club

Main Dining room hours: Tuesday through Friday, 11 a.m. - 2 p.m. Top of the Tower Dining Room: Tuesday through Thursday, 5 p.m. - 9 p.m. Friday and Saturday, 5 p.m. - 10 p.m. Closed on Sundays and Mondays
The Club will accommodate private parties during regular hours of operation. Special arrangements may be made for parties outside of normal Club hours with Club Manager.
Amenities: Finest food and service. Exquisite dining room and lounge. Panoramic view of the city. Special promotions. Five private suites seat up to 30. Starlight Room accommodates up to 150 people. Reciprocity at over 150 clubs throughout the world.
A Gentle Reminder: Please make reservations for lunch and dinner before coming to The Club. It helps us serve you better.

Bananas Foster

2 - 4 oz. scoops vanilla ice cream
3 Tbsp. butter
2 Tbsp. white sugar
Myers rum

1 banana (sliced 1/4 inch thick)
3 Tbsp. brown sugar
Cinnamon
Banana liquor

Melt 1/2 the butter in a skillet on medium heat and add brown and white sugar. When sugar begins to melt down (do not burn sugar), add bananas, and stir for 1/2 minute. Add cinnamon, Myers rum and cream de banana. Turn heat off and stir in remaining butter.

Serve over ice cream and garnish with whipped cream and sweet paste cookie.

Submitted by: Brad Lyons C.E.C. Executive Chef

Tuscan Grill

3631 E Sunshine St
Springfield, MO 65809
(417) 883-7800

www.parrinobros.com

Jay Parrino moved here from St. Louis in 1983, the year that he opened J. Parrinos' Pasta House and Bar on East Battlefield. Having been in the restaurant business here in Springfield since then, he has opened and operated different restaurants in the local market. In addition to the J. Parrinos locations in the Galleria on Battlefield and in the Heer's Building, Jay was also co-founder of the Pasta Express chain of carry-out pasta locations that have been operating since 1991. He has since sold all other concepts except Pasta Pronto on National. While most of the restaurants have had an Italian flavor to the cuisine, steaks and seafood are not out of his realm, or catering to large groups. His newest adventure is The Tuscan Grill, where besides Italian food; there are plenty of steak and chicken options to choose from.

The Tuscan Chocolate Cannelloni

1 - 13 oz. jar Nutella (chocolaty hazelnut spread)
1 pkg. Melissa's egg roll wraps (approx size 7 x 7 inch)
Frying oil (Crisco)

Add oil to pan till about several inches deep. Adjust heat for frying to 350°. Fill wraps with small amount of Nutella. Roll like a burrito, tucking ends in so the filling does not ooze out. Use water to seal edge. Fry until golden, about a minute or so. Plate with whipped cream, sprinkle with powdered sugar, add fresh berries or dip into Hershey's chocolate syrup.

Submitted by: Jay Parrino, Owner & Chef

17) It's All Downtown Trivia

Downtown Springfield offers which activities for families?

a. Rock-Climbing Wall

b. Vintage Video Games

c. Ice Skating

d. All of the above

Answer on page 200

INDEX

It's All Downtown Trivia – Answers

1. a 2. b 3. c 4. b 5. b 6. c 7. d 8. d 9. c
10. d 11. a 12. d 13. d 14. b 15. a 16. b 17. d